THE FACE OF GOD

The Face of God

The Gifford Lectures 2010

ROGER SCRUTON

continuum

Continuum International Publishing Group

The Tower Building	80 Maiden Lane
11 York Road	Suite 704
London	New York
SE1 7NX	NY 10038

www.continuumbooks.com

First published 2012
Reprinted 2012

British Library Cataloguing-in-Publication Data
A catalogue record for this book is available from the British Library.

ISBN: HB: 978-1-8470-6524-7

Library of Congress Cataloging-in-Publication Data
A catalog record for this book is available from the Library of Congress.

Typeset by Fakenham Prepress Solutions, Fakenham, Norfolk NR21 8NN
Printed and bound in Great Britain

Contents

List of Illustrations

Preface

This book contains the published version of the Gifford Lectures delivered in the University of St Andrews during the Spring of 2010. Lord Gifford's bequest was to sponsor public lectures in the Scottish Universities that would 'promote and diffuse ... the knowledge of God'. And he hoped that the lectures would be accessible without specialist expertise. I have therefore tried to avoid the technical details that academic philosophers might think to be essential to the proper development of my argument, and I have passed quickly over debates that seem to me to be marginal to the concerns of ordinary educated people.

I am grateful to the University of St Andrews for inviting me to give these lectures, and to the lively audiences who made it such a pleasure to deliver them. I am particularly grateful to Professor John Haldane of the department of philosophy, who took a leading part both in securing the invitation and in ensuring that it would be such a rewarding and pleasurable experience to accept it.

In preparing these lectures for publication I have filled in some of the arguments, but tried to maintain the relatively informal style in which they were first composed. Here and there I have added footnotes that will guide the interested reader to discussions that I have judged to be too specialized or intricate to deserve a place in the text. Previous versions have been read by John Cottingham, Fiona Ellis, Alicja Gęścińska and Raymond Tallis, and I am grateful to them for their comments and criticisms.

Malmesbury, June 2011

1

The View from Nowhere

Lord Gifford was not an orthodox adherent of any religion, but someone who nevertheless believed that our relation to God is the most important relation we have. He lived among people who shared that belief, and he himself assumed that philosophy, psychology and anthropology would confirm it. I doubt that he anticipated the culture that prevails today, in which the belief in God is widely rejected as a sign of emotional and intellectual immaturity. But I think he would have endorsed.the attempt to explore what we lose, when we lose that belief. And this will be one of my themes in what follows. I will be considering some of the consequences of the atheist culture that is growing around us: and I will suggest that it is not only an intellectual phenomenon, expressing a disbelief in God, but also a moral phenomenon, involving a turning away from God.

You might wonder how people can deliberately turn away from a thing that they believe not to exist. But God is in intimate relationship even with those who reject him. Like the spouse in a sacramental marriage, God is *unavoidable*, or avoidable only by creating a void. This void opens before us when we destroy the face – not the human face only, but also the face of the world. The godless void is what confronts us, when our surroundings are defaced. I do not deny that atheists can be thoroughly upright people, far better people than I am. But there is more than one motive underlying the atheist culture of our times, and the desire to escape from the eye of judgement is one of them. You escape from the eye of judgement by wiping away the face.

I begin from the scientific worldview, which many people believe is the real source of current doubts about the belief in God. According to Richard Dawkins, the most prominent of the evangelical atheists today, human beings are 'survival machines' in the service of their genes.[1] We are by-products of a process that is entirely indifferent to our wellbeing, machines developed by our genetic material and adapted by natural selection to the task of propagation. Genes themselves are complex molecules, put together in accordance with the laws of chemistry, from material made available in the primeval soup that once boiled on the surface of our planet. How it happened is not yet known: maybe electrical discharges caused nitrogen, carbon, hydrogen and oxygen atoms to link together in appropriate chains, until one of these chains achieved the remarkable feature that we know as life, but which is better described as the encoding of instructions for its own reproduction. Science may one day be able to answer the question how this occurred. But it is *science*, not religion, that will answer the question.

As for the existence of a planet, in which the elements abound in the quantities in which they abound on planet Earth, such a thing is again to be explained by science – though the science of astrophysics rather than the science of biology. The existence of the earth is part of a great unfolding process, set in motion by a Big Bang, which contains many mysteries that physicists explore with ever

1. See especially *The Blind Watchmaker: Why the Evidence of Evolution Reveals a Universe Without Design*, New York, Norton and Co., 1986.

increasing astonishment. Astrophysics has raised as many questions as it has answered. But they are scientific questions, to be answered by discovering the laws of motion that govern the observable changes at every level of the physical world, from galaxy to quark, and from black hole to supernova. The mystery that confronts us as we gaze upwards at the Milky Way, knowing that the stars crystallized in that smear of light are merely stars of a single galaxy, the galaxy that contains us, and that beyond its boundaries a myriad other galaxies turn in space, some dying, some emerging, all forever inaccessible to us and all receding at unimaginable speed – this mystery does not call for a religious response. For it is a mystery that results from our partial knowledge, and which can be solved only by further knowledge of the same kind – the knowledge that we call science. Perhaps, if the Big Bang theory is correct, there was a moment when this all began. But what was true at that moment is in principle unknowable to us, the laws of physics operating only from the moment an infinitesimal fraction of a second later (so-called Planck time), when the space–time continuum emerged.[2] To the question 'how were things at the beginning?' there is no intelligible answer; in which case maybe it is not an intelligible question. Indeed the concept of a *beginning*, implying a time *when* things began, is itself contentious, since it seems to imply that there could be a time outside the space–time continuum, a time when time had not emerged.

Only ignorance would cause us to deny the general picture painted by modern science, and many atheists today assume that monotheistic religion *must* deny that picture and therefore

---

2. Whether or not the Big Bang hypothesis adds to, or detracts from, the appeal of traditional cosmological arguments for the existence of God seems to me to be largely undecidable. See, for contrasting views, Richard Swinburne, *The Existence of God*, second edn, Oxford, Clarendon Press, 2004, and Herman Philipse, *God in the Age of Science: A Critique of Religious Reason*, Oxford, OUP, 2011, Part III.

must, at some level, commit itself to the propagation of ignorance or at any rate the prevention of knowledge. As for the atheists themselves, they typically deduce from the scientific worldview two far-reaching metaphysical doctrines. First, that everything in the natural world, human thought and action included, happens in accordance with scientific laws, so that the same laws govern events in the atom and events in the galaxy, events in the ocean and events in the mind. Secondly, that everything that happens is *contingent*. There is no reason that it should happen, other than the fact that it happens, in the sequence dictated by the laws of nature. There is no final explanation of *why* the world exists: it just does. Indeed, there is something incoherent about the question 'why?' asked of the existence of the world. We can, by observation and experiment, arrive at explanations of one event in terms of others. And we can link event to event in a continuous causal chain. But the idea that we can step outside the chain of events, and ask for an explanation of *it* is like the idea that we can see beyond the edge of our visual field, and so set a limit to it.

The argument was developed by Kant in the 'Antinomies' chapter of the *Critique of Pure Reason*, and it has haunted philosophy ever since. At some point we are compelled to accept that *this is how things are*, and that explanations are at an end. Any attempt to see the world as a whole, so as to find an explanation of *it*, is doomed to failure: indeed, Kant thought, it must end in contradiction. It could succeed only if we could think outside the limits of our own thinking, and attain to the 'transcendental' perspective that is God's. From that perspective it is conceivable that a proof of God's existence could be given; but necessarily it is a perspective that could never be ours. That Kantian argument has the interesting corollary that only God could ever prove God's existence; for only God can occupy the position outside the space–time continuum from which the ultimate ground of contingent things could be known.

We can summarize the atheist picture, therefore, in two doctrines: that everything happens in accordance with the laws of nature; and that those laws are contingent, summarizing the way things are, and being without any further explanation. We know that the universe is without a plan and without a goal – not because we have looked for those things and failed to find them, but because nothing discoverable to science could count as a plan or a goal for the universe in its entirety. Plans and goals are biological features of individual organisms, which are systems within the on-going stream of physical events, just like everything else.

It is not easy to be satisfied with a worldview that maintains those two positions. Surely, we feel, the law-governed nature of the universe requires an explanation. We may not phrase the question in religious terms, but there is, nevertheless, a question: *why* is the universe governed by comprehensible laws? If all is contingent, then why is it not also random? One response to this question has been to argue for the extreme unlikelihood of a law-governed universe, containing creatures like us. Several recent thinkers have emphasized that the alteration by a tiny fraction of the fundamental constants of physics would lead to a universe from which life and consciousness are forever excluded. Therefore, they have concluded, it is so improbable that just *this* universe should exist that we must suppose some divine intelligence as its cause.[3] Such arguments are, however, empty. We can speak of probability only where we can make comparative judgements or statistical calculations. Given one and only one universe, such judgements and calculations cannot be made; assertions of probability and likelihood are therefore groundless.

---

3. See, for example, Richard Swinburne, 'Argument from the Fine-Tuning of the Universe', in John A. Leslie (ed.), *Physical Cosmology and Philosophy*, New York, Macmillan, 1990, pp. 160–87. This and similar proposals are criticized by Elliott Sober, in 'The Design Argument', in W. Mann (ed.), *The Blackwell Companion to Philosophy of Religion*, Oxford, Blackwell, 2004, pp. 117–47.

Another response is contained in the so-called 'weak anthropic principle', which holds that if the universe were random it would also be unknowable, since it is only in a law-governed universe, and one very like this one, that creatures capable of *knowledge* could exist. Knowledge is, after all, a highly delicate condition, whereby states of affairs are causally connected to their own mental representation. Such a condition presupposes far-reaching law-like connections. Hence, if we can look for explanations at all, the universe cannot be random, but must be governed by finely tuned laws. It does not 'so happen' that the universe is law-governed. If it were not so, we could not know that it were not so.[4]

The suggestion recalls the 'transcendental idealism' of Kant. The world, Kant argued, must satisfy the *a priori* requirements of the understanding. It must be ordered in space and time, and it must conform to the 'categories' – to those concepts like substance and cause without which we could not make judgements. Those concepts can be meaningfully used only if certain principles are true of the world to which they are applied. Hence we can know *a priori* that the world obeys those principles, which are the pre-conditions of knowledge. One of these principles is the law of causality – the law that every event has a cause. Hence the truth of this law is not merely contingent. It is a matter of 'synthetic *a priori*' knowledge.

I think it is fair to say that Kant did not succeed in carrying that argument to the conclusion that he wanted. The best

---

4. For discussions of this principle see Stephen Hawking, 'The Cosmological Constant and the Weak Anthropic Principle', in M. J. Duff and C. J. Isham (eds), *Quantum Structure of Space and Time*, Cambridge, CUP, 1982, pp. 423–37, and *A Brief History of Time: From the Big Bang to Black Holes*, New York, Bantam Dell, 1988; and B. Carter, 'Large Number Coincidences and the Anthropic Principle in Cosmology', in M. S. Longair (ed.), *Confrontation of Cosmological Theories with Observational Data*, Dordrecht, Reidel, 1974, pp. 291–8.

that he could prove is that the world must appear ordered if we are to make judgements about it. But this is not so much a fact about the world as a fact about us. The question I am pursuing is rather different from the one that occupied Kant, namely: why, to what end, and for what reason, do we live in a law-governed world? It may be that any other world would not be a world that contains creatures like us, who can ask the kinds of question that I am asking here and now. But then, why, to what end, and for what reason, is there a world that contains creatures like us?

When theologians first attempted to confront the scientific revolution of the seventeenth century, it was in the context of the Newtonian picture of physical reality, as contained within a static Euclidean frame. Space and time were conceived as absolute, unchangeable, the background against which the drama of 'motion and rest' plays itself out. Einstein's general theory of relativity brought space and time into the foreground; they became part of the causal network, matrices which change with the things they contain. Meanwhile quantum mechanics disturbed the foundations of physics, predicting that the condition of one particle might be linked to that of another, even though no force can pass between them, a result that Einstein could not accept and against which he knocked his great head in vain.[5] In the world of quantum mechanics what is and what is knowable seem to melt into each other, like characters in fiction, who are not truly distinct from their stories. The Newtonian universe, which seemed such a robust toy in the Creator's hand, dissolves at the upper level into fluctuations of the space–time continuum, and at the lower level into ungrounded probabilities, statements about what can

5. See the debates around the Einstein–Podolsky–Rosen thought experiment and the 'Bell inequality': I explain some of the issues here in *Modern Philosophy: An Introduction and Survey*, London, Sinclair-Stevenson, 1994, pp. 223–5.

be measured, from which the things themselves have all but disappeared.

And the worst of it is that, while the theory of relativity and quantum mechanics have both been confirmed again and again, the two have not been unified, and in the effort to bring them together physicists have produced ever more bizarre and counter-intuitive descriptions of the physical world. Some believe that a unified physics will be delivered by string theory, with its nine-dimensional space, and its arbitrary-seeming constants. Some propose a 'multiverse', according to which our universe is merely one contender for a reality that is distributed across an indefinite number of alternative worlds. Whatever line we take, it is clear that while science has closed the gap between the world and our knowledge, it has also dissolved the world in the knowledge. By becoming knowable the world has ceased to be imaginable. We live within a vast mathematical conundrum, only a tiny corner of which makes proper sense to us. And if God exists, could he have intended so bewildering a thing?

Not surprisingly, therefore, the relevance of scientific expla-nation to the claims of theology has become totally unclear. Dawkins writes as though the theory of the selfish gene puts paid once and for all to the idea of a creator God – we no longer need that hypothesis in order to explain how we came to be. In a sense that is true. But what about the gene itself: how did that come to be? What about the primordial soup? Those questions are answered by going one step further down the chain of causation. But at each step we encounter a world with a singular quality: namely that it is a world which, left to itself, will produce conscious beings, able to look for the reason and the meaning of things, as well as for the cause. The astonishing thing about our universe – that it contains rational consciousness, judgement, the knowledge of right and wrong, and all the other things that make the human condition so singular – is not rendered less astonishing by the hypothesis that this state of affairs emerged over time from other conditions. If true, that merely shows us how astonishing those other conditions were. The gene and the soup cannot be less astonishing than their product; and the fact that it was to evolve in *this* direction, towards a world that had obtained consciousness of itself, was surely the most puzzling feature of that dense packet of stuff that emerged 10^{-43} seconds after the Big Bang. But is this astonishment just a blank astonishment, one that can never be solaced with an explanation?

Some help can be gained by turning to the question that causes all our problems: the question 'why?'. Aristotle argued that this question can be answered in four different ways, and that each way of answering it introduces a different kind of cause. His theory of the four causes was swept aside by the scientific worldview, which recognizes only one kind of cause – what Aristotelians call the 'efficient' cause – and one kind of law, which is the mathematically expressed connection of quantities, joining cause to effect.

Nevertheless, Aristotle was right in one respect. It is in the nature of consciousness to ask other kinds of 'why?' from those posed by the scientist. We are not satisfied with the 'why?' of causal explanation. We strive to see things from outside and as a whole. We are troubled by the 'why?' of reason, and also by the 'why?' of meaning. What *reason* is there for the world's existence, and what does this existence mean? The 'why?' of reason is not necessarily looking for a purpose; but it is seeking an account that removes the paradox of an entirely law-governed world, open to consciousness, that is nevertheless without an explanation: that just *is*, for no reason at all. And the 'why?' of meaning is not looking for a translation. It is seeking an *account*, a *logos*, which relates object to subject as a smile relates you to me. In this sense you might ask for the meaning of a motif in architecture, of a chord in music, of a colour in painting – not seeking the equivalent in words, for there is no equivalent, but seeking the

contexts and comparisons that put you at ease with the thing
that puzzles you.

The theologians of the Middle Ages drew inspiration
from the strange, stark theology contained in Aristotle's
Metaphysics, and in the theological arguments of the Muslim
Kalam – the early school of theology that regarded reason as
a sufficient foundation for religious truth.[6] Aristotle believed
that motion requires an explanation, and that therefore
there must be an unmoved mover who makes the world go
round. This unmoved mover acts on the world not as an
efficient cause but as a final cause – in other words, not as
the mechanical producer of motion but as the object towards
which all motion tends, as an action tends towards its goal.
God moves the world as the beloved moves the lover: so
Aristotle expressed the point. And this universal object of love
has both life and thought. It is a spirit on the ultimate edge
of things, which exists eternally, as both the subject and the
object of an unending contemplation.

Aristotle's view raises in a vivid way the question that I
wish to discuss in what follows, which is the question of
God's presence. How can such a being as Aristotle describes
take an interest in, be revealed to or be in any way related
to us in this world? This question becomes even more vivid
when we turn to the arguments of the medieval philosophers, and in particular to that introduced by Avicenna from
contingent being.

This argument is a metaphysical reconfiguration of
Aristotle's argument for the Prime Mover. It was designed to
show that the contingent being of anything at all is explicable
only on the assumption that being is not always contingent
– in other words that there is a necessary being. The task
of theology was thereafter conceived as that of explicating

6. See Harry Austryn Wolfson, *The Philosophy of the Kalam*, Cambridge, Mass.,
Harvard University Press, 1976.

the concept of a necessary being. What else must be true of something, if it is to exist necessarily and not contingently? To the delight of the monotheists of the Middle Ages the attributes of the necessary being, as they unfolded in thought, coincided with those attributed in the Torah, the Gospels and the Koran to the one God.[7] It is worth pausing to consider how Avicenna arrived at this conclusion.[8]

Being, Avicenna argued, is caught in three predicaments: there are impossible beings (those whose definition involves a contradiction), contingent beings (those which might not have existed) and necessary beings. The contingent being has the potentiality both to be and not to be, without contradiction. You and I are contingent beings in that sense, and even if I am granted a certain intuition of my own existence, that certainty is merely a personal possession and neither guarantees my survival, nor refutes the view that there are possible worlds in which I am not.

A necessary being is one that is 'true in itself' – in other words, whose existence follows from its nature – whereas a contingent being is 'false in itself' and owes its truth to other things – in other words, is contingent upon the thing that causes or sustains it. The necessary being has no essence (*mahiyya*, or 'whatness') other than existence itself. Hence it cannot be distinguished from others of its supposed kind, all of which are identical with it. The necessary being therefore is one (*waHid*): a point later taken up by Spinoza and used to argue that nothing exists *except* the one necessary being, but connected by Avicenna with that central concept in all Islamic

---

7. Whether those attributes – omniscience, omnipotence, benevolence and eternity – are consistent with one another is a question that I must pass over. For sceptical views see Anthony Kenny, *The God of the Philosophers*, Oxford, OUP, 1979; and J. L. Mackie, *The Miracle of Theism: Arguments For and Against the Existence of God*, Oxford, OUP, 1982.
8. For the sources, and another version of the argument, see Lenn E. Goodman, *Avicenna*, updated edn, Ithaca, Cornell University Press, 2005.

thinking, the concept of *tawHîd*, which means recognizing, in heart and mind and soul, the essential and creative oneness of God, the oneness of a thing that belongs to no kind since it can be circumscribed by no classification.

Avicenna argued that since all contingent beings are contingent upon some other thing to which their existence is owed, there must be a necessary being on which they all depend. Avicenna argued for this in one way, Aquinas, taking up the argument, in another.[9] Suppose, Aquinas argues, that there is no necessary being, and that all beings might not have been. Since time, in which all contingencies occur, is infinite (there being, on the hypothesis, no being who can set limits to it) then it is true of any contingent being that there will be some time at which it is not; and therefore some time at which all contingent beings are not – a time of utter nothingness. But this null point of the universe must already have existed, since past time, like future time, is infinite. And since nothing can arise out of nothing, then there would, from that point, be forever nothing. But there is something – namely this thing, which is pondering the question of being. So the hypothesis must be false, which means that there *is*, after all, the necessary being on which all other things depend. And this thing is – to adapt Avicenna's language – *causa sui* (*wajib al-wujud bi-dhatihi*); it is dependent on itself, the sustainer of everything. And it is *one* thing, a unity, admitting, in the words of the Koran, 'no partners'.

One of the many insights that are contained in this argument, and all the subtle (if at times tedious) metaphysics that flowed from it in the medieval schools, is the implication that the world of contingent beings, to which we belong, is governed by its own laws, the laws of generation and passing away. We discover those laws through scientific investigation, and they are the laws of nature that bind us all. They

9. *Summa theologiae*, I, 2–3.

include those laws of genetics which, in the view of Dawkins, provide a final refutation of the belief in God. But, according to Avicenna, there is another relation of dependence than the one explored by science: the relation of the contingent to the necessary, of the world to its 'sustainer' (*rabb*, to use the Koranic term, meaning 'master' or 'the one ultimately in charge'), and this is not a relation subject to empirical enquiry, nor one that can be known or refuted by scientific advance.

The relation of dependence that binds the world to God gives the reason why things are as they are. But this reason is not a cause: causes are the subject matter of science and are spelled out by the universal laws that we discover through experiment and observation. The causal relation is a relation in time, which binds temporal (and therefore contingent) entities. In referring to the ultimate reason of things we are dealing with another kind of answer to the question 'why?' and another meaning of *therefore*. And this is what gives sense to the life of prayer. We do not suppose that God can be summoned to our aid at every instance, or that he is waiting in the wings of nature, dealing out the cards. If we take the ideas behind Avicenna's argument seriously then we move towards another idea of God than that which informs the superstitious mind. God's freedom is revealed in the laws that bind us, and by which he too is bound, since it would be a loss of God's freedom, and not a gain, were he to defy the laws that govern the created world, and which spell out his Providence. But this does not mean that God is beyond our reach. He is in and around us, and our prayers shape our personal relation with him. We address him, as we address those we love, not with the 'why?' of explanation, but with the 'why?' of reason and the 'why?' of meaning. We want to know the end and the meaning, as well as the cause, and to school ourselves in the discipline of acceptance. It is this posture, rather than any belief in supernatural interventions, that forms the religious worldview – the posture of submission, or *islâm*.

I used to be very sceptical of those old arguments, largely for the reason spelled out by Kant, who pointed out that they involve the attempt to go beyond the limits of scientific thinking, and to apply concepts like 'cause', 'substance', 'probability' and 'quality' to the world conceived as a whole, rather than to the empirically encountered items within it. There is, Kant suggested, always an illegitimate leap from the realm of understanding – in which we apply our thinking to experience, in order to know the world as it presents itself to us – to the realm of pure reason, in which we are tempted to ask questions that have no answer since they apply concepts outside the domain in which they make real distinctions. Just such a question is the one I have been considering – the question 'why?' asked of the world as a whole.

Kant, however, was very ambivalent towards his own conclusion. He took the view that the tendency of reason to overstep the bounds of science is both incorrigible and inevitable. The question 'why?' will not go away, just because of a philosophical theory that condemns it as illegitimate. For it is a question that bears on our most fundamental anxiety – the anxiety of existence itself. 'Why am I?' is a question that you may dismiss, as a question without an answer. But by so dismissing it, you also answer it, in something like the way that Sartre answered it in his early 'existentialist' writings. By saying that there is no answer to the question 'why am I?' you invite the thought that your own existence is a kind of absurdity; and from that thought it is a small step to the existentialist conclusion, that there *is* a reason for your existence, but it is up to you, and you alone, to provide it. Such an existentialist answer then reinforces the question, which imposes itself day after day, and minute after minute, in our personal lives.

If you accept Avicenna's argument from contingent being, then you must also accept that the relation of dependence between God and the world is not a causal relation – that

is to say it is not a special case of those law-like connections between contingent events that we know through the
methods of empirical science. The 'God of the philosophers'
is not an empirical but a transcendental being: one whose
nature and being place him outside the world of empirical
particulars, sustaining that world in some way, but not in
the way that a pillar holds up a beam or in the way that a
mother supports her child. It then becomes hard to envisage
how such a being, whose nature is eternally the same, could
intervene in the world at all.[10] We seem, indeed, to be forever
and irremediably cut off from him – he becomes the *deus
absconditus*, the hidden God, as Aquinas described him. And
how can we relate to such a God: how can we love him or
know that he loves us in return? If we resolve the tension
between the theistic and the scientific worldview in Avicenna's
way, then the danger is that we end up with an unknowable
and unlovable God – since only what is knowable can be
truly loved. And if that is so, how can we obey the two great
commandments, to love God entirely and our neighbour as
ourselves, the commandments, as Christ said, on which 'hang
all the law and the prophets'? This problem occurs not merely
for the God of Avicenna, but also for the God of Averroës,
the God of Moses Maimonides, even the God of Aquinas.
For the problem arises precisely because we have set out to
prove God's existence from purely abstract premises, and
without reference to how things are in the empirical world.
The argument with which we hope to answer science ends by
hiding God.

We are pushed, therefore, towards a troubling question:
what use to us is this transcendental being about whom
nothing can be known except that he lies beyond knowledge?
How can we partake of the view from nowhere that is
God's? How can we pray to such a God, and how can

10. See the argument in Kenny, *op. cit.*

we make room for him in our lives, as one makes room for a spouse or a friend? Surely God must be present *in* the world, if we are to have faith in him: for faith is a personal relation, a relation of trust, that demands the kind of mutuality that one free being can offer to another, in the world of space and time.

Now, if the belief in God were nothing more than a piece of abstract metaphysics, it is hard to see that it would matter whether we believe or disbelieve. Science plus metaphysics is the equivalent of science, when it comes to real and practical decisions. But there is another aspect to religious belief, one that has been of far greater interest to anthropologists and psychologists than the abstruse reasoning of the philosophers. It has been evident since Durkheim's great essay on *The Elementary Forms of the Religious Life* that religions exist and endure in part because they offer membership.[11] You are born into a faith, or converted to it; and you may find it difficult to leave without an existential catastrophe. In some cases, such as Islam, you are *forbidden* to leave the faith – you may lapse into a state of ignorance or *jahiliyya*, but conversion to another faith is a negation of what you truly *are*, and therefore an inner path to the death sentence that is the outward expression of your fall. So this raises a new question: how can *belief* be a form of membership? The simple answer is that belief is a form of membership when it defines a community. By signing up to the doctrine you are incorporated into the community. And this incorporation is regularly reaffirmed through sacred rites that signify, in some way, the collective relation of the community to its God.

It is, of course, absurd to think in that way of scientific beliefs, which offer nothing by way of membership and indeed nothing save themselves, along with the challenge to refute

11. Émile Durkheim, *Les formes élémentaires de la vie religieuse*, Paris, F. Alcan, 1912.

them – a challenge which, according to Popper's plausible view of things, is integral to their claim to be science.[12] Indeed, when a system of beliefs begins to persecute those who do not accept it, we know – or ought to know – that it is only a pseudo-science. That surely is transparently obvious in the case of Freudianism and Marxism, two so-called sciences that turned the world upside down by laying claim to the souls, rather than the reasoned opinions, of their followers.

I think it is this fact about religion, far more than any apparent conflict between its doctrines and the theories of science, which explains the sense that somehow religion and science are at odds with each other. If a belief offers membership then it has to be protected in some way – the destiny of a human community has been bound up with it, and the defence of the belief is the defence of that community. This explains the concept of heresy, and why heretics are so severely treated by traditional religions. It explains why heretics are more fiercely perse-cuted the smaller their deviation from orthodoxy – deviate far enough and you are not part of the community, so that your beliefs can be ignored. Deviate by an inch and you threaten the community from within. Thus the seventeenth-century Polish theologian Jan Crell remarked on the contrast between the intolerance of Catholic establishments towards heretics, and their easy-going acceptance of the Jews and Muslims with whom they did business, and whose 'blasphemies against Christ' the Catholics peacefully ignored.[13]

This is the aspect of religion which, I think, most troubles those religious people who have a respect for scientific method,

12. Sir Karl Popper, *The Logic of Scientific Discovery*, 1934, English edn (Routledge), 1959.
13. See *A Learned and Exceeding Well Compiled Vindication of Liberty of Religion*, London, 1646, the English translation of Crell's Latin, Chapter 2. Crell was a leading member of the Polish Brethren (the Socinians), and a powerful influence on John Locke. See Sarah Mortimer, *Reason and Religion in the English Revolution: The Challenge of Socinianism*, Cambridge, CUP, 2010.

and who have absorbed the lessons – the very many lessons – of the Enlightenment, wishing to follow the path of 'religion within the limits of reason alone', as Kant expressed it in the title of his book on this subject – a book which got him into trouble with the censors precisely because it seemed to chase God from his familiar haunts in the empirical world. How can we reconcile the community-forming nature of religious beliefs with their claims to truth? Are we, through faith, rescuing belief from refutation, and how can that be done without destroying its nature as a genuine belief, something that might be true or false, depending on the evidence?

Under the influence of Wittgenstein and Quine, philosophers sometimes advocate a third-person approach to the theory of knowledge, describing our epistemological capacities as features of the natural world. Those things really exist, they argue, which are referred to in the *true explanation* of our beliefs. For example, our beliefs about the physical world are best explained by assuming that the physical world exists, in the form that science describes, and that we have evolved so as to gain accurate information about its contours. True beliefs are causally connected to their subject matter in ways that facilitate our dealings. False beliefs result from 'deviant causal chains', as in the case of hallucinations, which break the connection between representation and reality.

This approach has radical implications for theology. If the usual claims of faith are true, God is transcendental. He is not part of nature and not a possible object of scientific enquiry. No scientific explanation of religious belief could possibly refer to him. It follows that, if there *is* an explanation, it will be 'naturalistic': it will explain religious belief in terms of forces and functions that make no reference to God. The best explanation of our belief in the transcendental can make no reference to the transcendental. Does it follow that the belief is unfounded? Perhaps not. For the existence of such a naturalistic explanation is precisely what God's existence would entail. (Compare our belief in the existence of numbers. Our mathematical beliefs are not caused by numbers, which are abstract objects, without causal powers. Yet many of our beliefs about numbers are true.)

Whence, then, does religious belief arise? How, and in response to what thoughts or experiences, does it change? And the simple and straightforward answer seems to be the right one. Religious belief is received from a community – typically the community into which you are born – and it changes in response to changes in that community. Of course, it is also embellished by doctrine, and developed by rational enquiry. But the results of this enquiry become accepted into the religion only when the community has re-shaped itself around them. And this re-shaping of a community does not usually occur without violence, of the kind that blew Europe apart during the seventeenth century.

Science might attempt to explain religious belief in some such way. Religion, the evolutionary psychologist might say, is an adaptation which promotes our ability to stand together, to claim and defend our territory, and to make the kinds of sacrifice that are needed for collective survival, and therefore for our own survival, as beneficiaries of the inclusive bond.[14] The nature and scope of such evolutionary explanations is a matter to which I return. But we should not over-emphasize them. Adaptations are themselves adapted; and in human beings the process of adaptation proceeds rapidly and in a way that has no precedent among the lower animals. Moreover, we are rational animals, who furnish our biological needs with a justifying commentary. Hence for us life with religion differs at every level from life without it. This is something that needs to be repeatedly reaffirmed, not least because the illusion

14. See David Sloan Wilson, *Darwin's Cathedral: Evolution, Religion and the Nature of Society*, Chicago, University of Chicago Press, 2002.

persists among enlightened thinkers that religion consists merely in a set of beliefs, long ago disproved by science, but clung to nevertheless for the comfort that they afford.

In almost every religion, in addition to shared sacraments and acts of worship, there are the openings to, and the consolations of, solitude. The ascetic and the anchorite, the solitary pilgrim and the contemplative, seek another communion – that with God himself, with the world-spirit, with Brahman, or the Friend. These solitary off-shoots of the original religious urge have enormous importance in every serious faith, since they offer a way out of society which is another way into it. They look like a rejection of the world; but it is the world that creates the path to them. And through the discipline of self-denial the saint or the *bodhisattva* re-works the primal experience of community as a relation between himself and the transcendent meaning of the world.

The connection between belief in God and the community of believers is recognized in the Christian concept of communion. And this connection, far from casting doubt on the validity of transcendental theology, points the way to supplying what it lacks. The communion is the real presence of God among us, and it is from such acts of participation that we come to see who God is and how he relates to us. It is through the communion that we come face to face with God. In other words what is, from the scientific view, a defect in religious belief – namely that it has the authority of a community – is from the theological point of view a strength. For it is this connection with the community that enables us to bridge the gap opened by the arguments of the philosophers, and to find the transcendental God that is allegedly proved by those arguments as a real presence in our world. This, it seems to me, is the true meaning of the Christian Eucharist, and one reason why the meaning of that sacrament is so easy to experience, and so hard to explain – unless we explain it through a work of art, as Wagner did in *Parsifal*.

I shall argue that we can reconcile the God of the philosophers with the God who is worshipped and prayed to by the
ordinary believer, provided we see that this God is understood
not through metaphysical speculations concerning the ground
of being, but through communion with our fellow humans.
The religious community adapts the view from nowhere that
is God's to the view from somewhere that is ours. We can
justify this, I maintain, by exploring more fully the meaning
of three critical words: 'I', 'you' and 'why?' And in exploring
those words I shall be constructing a general theory of the
face: the face of the person, the face of the world, and the
face of God.

2

The View from Somewhere

I have suggested that the arguments that we might use to reconcile belief in God with the scientific worldview, however cogent in themselves, raise another problem for the believer, which is the problem of God's presence in the world. Where do we find him and how? The ghost of an answer to that question is this: God is a person, and he reveals himself as persons do, through a dialogue involving those three critical words, 'I', 'you' and 'why?'.[1] That answer brings us up against another problem raised by the scientific worldview, which is the problem of reconciling our beliefs about persons with the science of the human being.

Whatever philosophers have to say, their theories must fit in to the basic truth, which is that we are organisms, distinguished from other species by our cerebral capacity, which has permitted adaptations of an order that no other species has been able to match. These adaptations include language,

---

1. Christians believe that God is *three* persons in one substance, though the word 'person' in this use should be seen as a technical term, deriving from St Augustine's use of *persona* to translate the Greek *hypostasis* (*De Trinitate*). How we elucidate this technical term will depend in part on how we elucidate the *ordinary* meaning of the term 'person', which is one of my tasks in what follows.

social emotions, and cooperative strategies that range well beyond the demands of 'inclusive fitness'. They are what principally need to be understood by philosophers interested in the human condition. And they are understood, in the first instance, by exploring the context in which they evolved, and the evolutionary problems to which they are the solutions. Hence the growing body of literature in which evolutionary biologists, anthropologists, sociologists, political scientists and philosophers work side by side to postulate the roots of our human attributes in the daily emergencies of Pleistocene man.[2] Most contributors to this literature insist that they are not reductionists: that is, they are not trying to reduce human behaviour to something simpler than it is. They are tracing highly complex adaptations to the circumstances that selected them, in order to understand why and how those adaptations were acquired. And this must surely cast light on how they work for us, here, now, even if those circumstances have since disappeared.

This approach promises to dispel some of the mystery of the human condition. If some feature of our mental life can be shown to be an adaptation rooted in the tribulations of our hunter-gatherer past, then a bridge has been created between the peculiarities of civilized people, and the circumstances of the ape-like creatures from whom we are descended. What might otherwise appear to be an impassable gulf in the natural order, between the instinctive animal and the fully acculturated moral being, begins to look more like a step-by-step transition, each step being explicable in

2. See, for example, Robert Axelrod, *The Evolution of Cooperation*, New York, Basic Books, 1984; John Tooby and Leda Cosmides, 'The Psychological Foundations of Culture', in Jerome Barkow, Leda Cosmides and John Tooby (eds), *The Adapted Mind: Evolutionary Psychology and the Generation of Culture*, Oxford, OUP, 1992; Dan Sperber, *Explaining Culture*, Oxford, Blackwell, 1996; Elliott Sober and John Sloan Wilson, *Unto Others: The Evolution and Psychology of Unselfish Behaviour*, Cambridge, Mass., Harvard University Press, 1999.

evolutionary terms. By contrast, the *a priori* method of traditional philosophy paints a picture of the human condition
as something wholly apart from the rest of nature, as in the
philosophy of Kant, for whom the concept of the person is
central, but who writes of persons in such a way that it is
doubtful, in the end, whether they are part of the natural
world at all. For what distinguishes us as persons, according
to Kant, is our 'transcendental freedom', which we know for
certain, but cannot understand.

However, when biologists try to develop an account of the
human being that is founded in the Darwinian picture of how
we came to be, all too often they end either by describing us
as far simpler than we are, or by describing the lower animals
as far more complex than *they* are. This habit began with
Darwin, who writes thus in Chapter 3 of *The Descent of Man*:

> If ... men were reared under precisely the same conditions
> as hive-bees, there can hardly be a doubt that our unmarried
> females would, like the worker-bees, think it a sacred duty
> to kill their brothers, and mothers would strive to kill their
> fertile daughters; and no-one would think of interfering.[3]

That sentence forms part of an extended attempt to show
that the sentiments of people have their precise analogies
and archetypes in the animal kingdom, and that no special
explanatory leap need be made in order to describe the moral
sense, like the sense of beauty and the disposition to religion,
as an evolved response. But notice the implications: worker-
bees, in Darwin's view, do not merely have a sense of duty.
They possess the concept of the sacred too. They are fully
fledged Kantian persons, whose view of the world is exactly
the view that we should take, were we to enjoy the kind of

3. Charles Darwin, *Evolutionary Writings*, ed. James A. Secord, Oxford, OUP,
   2008, pp. 248–9.

boarding-school education that is provided in the hive. Darwin seems to be explaining the emergence of the moral sense from the instinctive social behaviour of animals by describing that behaviour as though it were already an instance of the moral sense. Such an explanation would be circular, concealing the mystery rather than solving it.

Consider further the 'explanations' of human benevolence in terms of 'reciprocal altruism', alleged to be an evolutionally stable strategy not just for human genes, but for the genes of any creature which can gain a reproductive benefit by doing something that benefits others. The origin of these explanations lies in the application of game theory to genetics by John Maynard Smith and to social evolution by Robert Axelrod, both popularized by Matt Ridley in *The Origins of Virtue*.[4] Ridley suggests that moral virtue is an adaptation, his evidence being that any other form of conduct would have set an organism's genes at a distinct disadvantage in the game of life. In the language of game theory, in the circumstances that have prevailed during the course of evolution, altruism is a dominant strategy.

Ridley's argument employs a minimalist conception of altruism, according to which an organism acts altruistically if it benefits another organism at a cost to itself. The concept applies equally to the soldier ant marching into the flames that threaten the anthill, and the officer who throws himself onto the live grenade that threatens his platoon. The concept of altruism, so understood, cannot explain, or even recognize, the distinction between those two cases. Yet the ant marches instinctively towards the flames, unable either to understand what it is doing or to fear the results of it, while the officer consciously lays down his life for his friends.

4. Robert Axelrod, *The Evolution of Cooperation*, New York, Basic Books, 1984; J. Maynard Smith and G. R. Price, 'The Logic of Animal Conflict', *Nature*, 246, 1973, 15–18; Matt Ridley, *The Origins of Virtue: Human Instincts and the Evolution of Cooperation*, London and New York, Viking (Penguin), 1991.

Rational beings have a motive to sacrifice themselves, regardless of genetic advantage. This motive would arise, even if the normal result of following it were that which the Greeks observed with awe at Thermopylae, or our ancestors at the Battle of Maldon. In such instances an entire community embraces death, in full consciousness of what it is doing, because death is the only honourable option. Even if you don't think Kant's account of this is the right one – say because you prefer Aristotle's, or because some other moral theory seems more plausible to you – the fact is that this motive is universally observed in human beings, and is entirely distinct from that of the soldier ant, in being founded on a consciousness of duty, and of the cost of performing it. The moral motive is essentially *inter-personal*: the one who is moved to do right, regardless of the cost of it, is seeing his own action from outside, as he would see the action of another, as an action that is binding on him.

On the approach of the evolutionary psychologists, the conduct of the Spartans at Thermopylae is over-determined. The 'dominant reproductive strategy' explanation, and the 'honourable sacrifice' explanation are both sufficient to account for what is done. So which is the real explanation? Or is the 'honourable sacrifice' explanation just a story that we tell ourselves, in order to pin medals on the chest of the ruined 'survival machine' that died in obedience to its genes?

Surely the moral explanation is genuine and sufficient. You cannot live life as we know it – the life of a person, accountable to others like oneself – without experiencing the force of moral norms. We may resist this motive; but only in pathological cases is it wholly absent. It follows that the genetic explanation is trivial. If rational beings are motivated to behave in this way, regardless of any genetic strategy, then that is sufficient to explain the fact that they do behave in this way. And, given the obvious social utility of this motive, we can conclude, without any reference to biology, that a competitor species, disposed to behave differently, would by now have died out.

Scientific explanations of the moral life often exhibit what I call the 'charm of disenchantment', the appeal that comes from wiping away the appearance of human distinctiveness. Take the thing that needs explaining – human generosity – find something that looks a bit like it – the alleged sharing of booty by the female vampire bat – and describe the animal behaviour in language appropriate to the human case (as a 'gift' to 'another') and for a brief moment it might look as though you have found the explanation.[5] The woman who gives her time and money to the local hospital is doing what the vampire bat has been alleged to do when she gives the blood she has collected to her less fortunate neighbour hanging beside her from the rafters. The soldier who lays down his life for his platoon and the ant who dies defending the ant-heap are doing exactly the same thing – acting out a successful reproductive strategy of the genes that compel them.

Such would-be explanations assimilate human to animal conduct only by giving the most superficial description of both. In particular they leave out of consideration the radically different *intentionality* of the human response. Human generosity is mediated by concepts like gift, sacrifice, duty, sanctity – concepts that presuppose the recognition of self and other and the sense, unique to rational beings, of being accountable for what we are and do, and therefore obliged to reflect on these things. The emergence of these concepts is what most needs explaining, since they create what seems like an impassable chasm in the evolutionary story. You don't cross that chasm merely by misdescribing the behaviour that creates it.

---

5. The blood-sharing behaviour of vampire bats is disputed; the evidence was originally set out by Gerald S. Wilson, 'Reciprocal Food Sharing in the Vampire Bat', *Nature*, 308, 181–4, 1984.

The evolutionary approach also fails to account for the internal logic of our states of mind. Consider mathematics. This too is an adaptation – if you can't add, you won't multiply. But you don't need much maths to satisfy the reproductive requirements of your genes, and someone who, in addition to carrying out basic calculations, becomes interested in transfinite cardinals and the topology of n-dimensional space is not giving much of a helping hand to the genetic strategies that brought him to this pass. Once over the hump, however, from an innumerate to a numerate creature, the human species was able to run forward into this new pasture, enjoying its wonderful fruit of futile knowledge, building theories and proofs, and in general transforming its vision of the world without any benefits to its reproductive potential – or with benefits that come far too late to exert any evolutionary pressure in favour of the research that produces them.

Stephen J. Gould and Richard C. Lewontin famously described this kind of activity as a 'spandrel' – on the analogy of those ornamented corners between architrave and arch, which serve no function and therefore can be decorated at will, without weakening the structure.[6] That, however, misrepresents the facts. Decoration is a free expression of personal choice, and is guided, but not determined, by what went before. Once into the domain of mathematics, by contrast, there is only one way you can go. Something constrains you, and it is not the clamorous demand of your genes for their useless immortality, but the constraints of validity and truth. We understand these constraints, because we understand reasoning. No evolutionary explanation is going to give us an account of *what* we understand. It can give us a causal map: but you could understand that map without understanding mathematics. And out of mathematical reasoning there arises

6. Stephen J. Gould and Richard C. Lewontin, 'The Spandrels of San Marco and the Panglossian Paradigm', *Proc. Roy. Soc. London* B 205, 1979, 581–98.

the *true* philosophical question, the question that no amount of biology could ever solve: namely, what is mathematics *about*? What in the world *are* numbers, sets and transfinite cardinals?

Nor is mathematics a special case. There are many ways in which people gain understanding of the world by interpreting signs and symbols, and even if there is an evolutionary explanation of how we came to acquire that kind of understanding, the understanding itself unfolds another vision of the world than that contained in the theory of evolution. Language is the most striking example of this. We don't know how it arose; the very idea of intermediate 'proto-languages' which are steps on the way from animal cries to articulate sentences has been seriously doubted (for example by Chomsky[7]). But we do know that language enables us to understand the world as no dumb animal could possibly understand it. Again there is a hump and a boundless field beyond it. Once over that hump, infinitely many representations are available; language users have access to the distinctions between truth and falsehood, between past, present and future, between possible, actual and necessary, and so on. It is fair to say that they live in another world from non-linguistic creatures. Since emotions and motives are founded on thoughts, their emotional life and their motives to act will be of an entirely different kind from those of the other animals. This is surely why we balk (or ought to balk) at those theories of altruism as an 'evolutionally stable strategy'. For altruism in people is not an instinctive thing. It is a considered response, based sometimes

7. In *Language and Mind*, Cambridge, MIT Press, 1968, and elsewhere. Some geneticists have advanced theories of 'proto-languages' which attempt to show both that there could be piecemeal advances towards linguistic competence, and that these advances would be selected at the genetic level. See, for example, John Maynard Smith and Eörs Szathmáry, *The Major Transitions in Evolution*, Oxford and New York, W. H. Freeman, 1995, pp. 303–8. But such theories never seem to negotiate the transition from correlations between words and things to rules of reference *from* words *to* things.

on *agape* or neighbour love, sometimes on complex inter-
personal emotions like pride and shame, which are in turn
founded on the recognition of the other as another like me.
In all cases altruism in people involves the recognition that
what is bad for *the other* is something that *I* have a motive
to remedy.

Such attitudes depend upon our ability to refer to ourselves
in the first person, and to use the pronoun 'I'. Thomas Nagel
has a nice way of expressing what this might involve. Imagine
a complete description of the world, according to the true
theory (whatever it turns out to be) of physics. This description
describes the disposition of all the particles, forces and fields
that compose reality, and gives spatio-temporal coordinates
for everything that is. Not a thing has been overlooked; and
yet there is a fact that the description does not mention, the
fact that is more important than any other to me – namely,
which of the things mentioned in the description am I? Where
in the world of objects am I? And what exactly is implied in
the statement that *this* thing is *me*?[8]

We tremble here on a vertiginous edge. The self is not a
thing but a perspective; but, as Nagel reminds us, perspectives
are not *in* the world but *on* the world. It is the distinction
of perspective between the first person and the third person
points of view that gives rise to many of the puzzles concerning
consciousness. When you judge that I am in pain it is on the
basis of my circumstances and behaviour, and you could be
wrong. When I ascribe a pain to myself I don't use any such
evidence. I don't find out that I am in pain by observation,
nor can I be wrong, except in special circumstances that are
immediately understood as abnormal. But that is not because
there is some *other* fact about my pain, accessible only to me,
which I consult in order to establish what I am feeling. For
if there were this inner private quality I could misperceive it:

8. Thomas Nagel, *The View from Nowhere*, Oxford, Clarendon Press, 1986.

I could get it wrong; and I would have to *find out* whether I am in pain. I would also have to invent a language, intelligible only to me, with which to describe my inner state – and that, Wittgenstein plausibly argued, is impossible. The conclusion to draw is that I ascribe pain to myself not on the basis of some inner characteristic but on no basis at all. There is no possibility of discovery here.[9]

Of course there is a difference between knowing what pain is and knowing what pain is *like*. But to know what it is like is not to know some additional inner *fact* about it: it is to retain the memory of 'how it felt'. We are dealing with familiarity rather than information. 'What it's like' is not proxy for a description, but a refusal to describe. This thought leads naturally to a distinction between the subject and the object of consciousness, and points to the peculiar metaphysical status of the subject. As a self-conscious subject I have a point of view on the world. The world *seems* a certain way to me, and this 'seeming' defines my unique perspective. Every self-conscious being has such a perspective, since that is what it means to be a subject, rather than a mere object. When I give a scientific account of the world, however, I am describing objects only. I am describing the way things are, and the causal laws that explain them. This description is given from no particular perspective. It does not contain words like 'here', 'now' and 'I'; and while it is meant to explain the way things seem, it does so by giving a theory of how they are.

In short, the subject is in principle unobservable to science, not because it exists in another realm but because it is not part of the empirical world. It lies on the edge of things, like a horizon, and could never be grasped 'from the other side', the side of subjectivity itself. Is it a real part of the real world?

9. I have in that paragraph summarized one aspect of Wittgenstein's famous private language argument. For a fuller exposition and reference to sources see my *Modern Philosophy, op. cit.*, Chapter 4.

The question begins to look as though it has been wrongly phrased. I refer to myself, but this does not mean that there is a self that I refer to. I act for the sake of my friend, but there is no such thing as a sake for which I am acting. Sakes are not objects in the world of objects. Neither are selves.

Kant wrote more beautifully of this matter than any other philosopher. The use of the word 'I', he suggested, distinguishes rational beings from all other objects in the natural world, and also defines their predicament as creatures both bound and free. Descartes had argued for the supreme reality of the self, as a unitary substance, whose nature is infallibly revealed to me by my introspective thoughts. That view, Kant argued, is profoundly flawed. For it tries to make the self into the object of its own awareness, one item among others in the empirical world. I know myself as *subject*, not as object. I stand at the edge of things, and while I can say of myself that I am this, here, now, those words contain no information about *what* I am in the world of space and time. Borrowing an idiom from Heidegger, J. J. Valberg argues that I am at the centre of a horizon, within which my experience plays itself out. And while I can know that others too exist, since thought requires language and language is essentially public and shared, I cannot enter the horizon of another, or reach beyond my horizon to the other's point of view.[10]

Yet there are two things that I know about myself as subject, and about which I cannot be mistaken, since any argument against them would presuppose their truth. The first is that I am a unified centre of consciousness. I know without observation that my present mental states – this thought, this sensation, this desire, and this intention – belong to one thing: and I know that this thing endures through time,

10. J. J. Valberg, *Dream, Death and the Self*, Princeton, Princeton University Press, 2007. I cannot in this short book do justice to the subtlety and beauty of Valberg's argument, but will say only that it touches at many points on my subject, and always in ways that illuminate its deeper significance.

and is subject to change. I am directly aware, as Kant put it, of the 'transcendental unity of apperception': the single unified owner of all my mental states. This privileged knowledge of my own present states of mind and of their common owner would be described by Wittgenstein as a 'grammatical' feature: a fact about the grammar of the first person case. But that is neither an explanation nor a denigration: it remains true that there is in each of us a sphere of self-knowledge that is privileged and that this sphere of self-knowledge defines the view from somewhere which is mine. Without that privileged sphere there would be no 'I': my world would be 'I-less', and therefore not mine or anyone's.

The second thing that I know with certainty is that I can give and receive reasons for action, judgement and belief. The question 'why?' makes sense to me, and when it is asked of my own beliefs, intentions or acts I can respond to it with the same authority with which I know my own state of mind. My beliefs may be wrong, my intentions evil and my feelings corrupt. But when you ask me to justify them it is I, not you, who give the reason why. There are difficult cases here, as we know from psychopathology. But the norm is certainty, and it is for just this reason that the 'why?' makes sense. Your 'why?' is a question that I can answer immediately, on no basis, at the same time offering myself for judgement. And because the answer to the question is, in that way, entirely within my grasp, your question is *addressed* to me – it seeks the I in me, as my answer seeks the I in you.

This feature of the human condition is both fundamental and mysterious. It is fundamental since it transfigures the human world, endows our actions with a significance that no animal activity can replicate, and makes it possible to describe human agents in ways that distinguish them completely from the surrounding world. It is mysterious in that there is nothing further to be said by way of explaining it: every creature who can say 'I' and thereby refer to himself is able to answer the question 'why?'. But there is nothing else about him that explains this fact.

Equally interesting is the second person case. We can observe and understand many things in our environment, and it is natural to seek an explanation for the things that we observe, asking 'why?' of the sun, the moon and the stars, of the weather, the landscape and the things that grow in it, and asking this too of the animals. But this 'why?' is not *addressed* to the things that we observe: we do not ask the sun to give an account of itself, or the trees to tell us how they grow. Of one thing in our environment, however, we ask 'why?' in another sense, and that is the thing we address as 'you'. I can address objects and animals as 'you', but only figuratively – certainly not using the word as we use it to each other, by way of calling each other to account for what we think and feel. 'How are you?' is usually the first thing that one person says to another; and it is a form of words that establishes a relation that can exist only between those who refer to themselves as I.

The I–You relation has received a certain amount of attention in modern philosophy, notably in a famous book by Martin Buber, *Ich und Du* (1923), and more recently in a carefully argued work by Stephen Darwall.[11] The I–You relation is both distinctive of persons and also constitutive of them. It is by addressing each other as 'you' that we bind ourselves in the web of inter-personal relations, and it is by virtue of our place in the web that we are persons. Personhood is a relational condition, and I am a person insofar as I can enter into personal relations with others like me. This may be a part of what Locke meant when he described the concept of the person as a 'forensic' concept:[12] it denotes the aspect of the human condition in which we assume responsibility for

11. Stephen Darwall, *The Second Person Standpoint: Respect, Morality and Accountability*, Cambridge, Mass., Harvard University Press, 2006.
12. John Locke, *An Essay Concerning Human Understanding*, 1689, Book IV.

our actions, account to each other for how things seem to us, provide reasons for our own and others' decisions, and praise and blame each other according to norms and aspirations that we strive to share. Hence the role of the second person case as a form of *address*, and not just a way of describing other people.

The word 'why?' has a special place in our inter-personal dialogue. When uttered face-to-face 'why?' has a particular expression, captured by Schumann in the little piece for piano, '*Warum?*'[13]: the question looks at you and into you. This inter-personal use is wholly different from the use of 'why?' in scientific explanation. Even if we respond to the question 'why?' by mentioning the cause of our state of mind we are also doing more than this. We are accounting for ourselves. And this accounting of self to other is also something that we do self to self, when we reflect on our actions and emotions in the spirit of judgement, seeing them from outside, as we see the actions and emotions of others. Contained in the question 'why?' is the remarkable fact that each of us is both self and other, bound to other persons in a network of face-to-face encounters. The question draws aside the veil that lies between us, to make a place where I stands looking into I.

Two important consequences follow from this. The first is that human beings can make up their minds to do one thing rather than another. An intention is not the same thing as a desire: you can intend to do what you don't want to do, and want to do what you don't intend to do. Intending something means being certain that you will do it, and being prepared to answer why. Intending is not predicting. I predict that I shall drink too much at the party tonight; but maybe the gods

13. The third of *Fantasiestücke*, op. 12. Vladimir Jankélévitch describes this 'why?' as an 'eternally suspended' question, since music has no answers. See *Music and the Ineffable*, trans. Carolyn Abbate, Princeton, Princeton University Press, 2003, p. 19.

will favour me and I shall find the strength to go home sober. When making such a prediction I am seeing myself from outside, as it were, assessing the evidence, extrapolating from past observations, and drawing conclusions as I would draw them from observing another. My prediction might turn out to be right or wrong: but it is no more privileged from the point of view of self-knowledge than my predictions about the behaviour of someone else.

When I *decide* to go home sober I 'make up my mind', and this means being certain, on no evidence, that that is what I shall do. In such a case I answer the question 'why?' not by presenting evidence based on past behaviour, but by offering *reasons for action*. I am *taking responsibility* for my future, and that means bringing it within the purview of first person knowledge, becoming certain that *that* is what I shall do. If I don't after all go home sober, this is not because I was mistaken in my former assertion about my future action, but because I changed my mind.

Ever since Aristotle's account of practical reasoning in the *Nicomachean Ethics*, philosophers have been troubled by the possibility of weakness of will – *akrasia*, as Aristotle called it. It seems that we sometimes decide to do something, and yet do not do it, even though nothing resembling a 'change of mind' occurs between the decision and the moment of weakness. How is this possible? The question takes us to the indecipherable edge of our being, the place where freedom and nature, subject and object, come apart. In weakness of will the plans of the subject, which nothing can defeat except a countervailing reason, are defeated without a reason. I cannot resolve this paradox: but what I say may to some extent blunt its impact.[14]

14. The paradox is emphasized by Donald Davidson, in an article that has generated an extensive literature. See 'How is Weakness of Will Possible?' (1969), collected in *Essays on Actions and Events*, second edn, Oxford, Clarendon Press, 2001.

The second consequence of the use of 'why?', therefore, is that human beings are rational agents: we act for reasons, and are open to criticism when our reasons seem inadequate or flawed. The question 'why?' lifts our actions out of the realm of cause and effect and places them squarely in the realm of reasons and goals. This is, in part, what we mean by calling an action intentional – namely, that it lies within the perspective of practical reason. The agent can be called to account for it, and is able spontaneously to answer the question 'why?' Some intentional actions are preceded by a decision: but not all are like that. As Elizabeth Anscombe has argued, an action is intentional just so long as it admits the application of 'a certain sense of the question "why?"' – the sense that I am considering in this chapter.[15] Hence an action can be intentional even if no decision preceded it: most of our actions are like that.

There are many qualifications and caveats to be added to that picture, but for the purposes of my argument they must be left to one side, since I need to give an overview of what it means for us, that the three metaphysical words, 'I', 'you' and 'why', govern our conduct and impose their own comprehensive orientation towards the world. We face the world in a posture of accountability. We are called upon to justify our conduct, to be truthful in revealing our states of mind and our goals, and to be aware of the community that stands as though on a balcony above our projects, expecting us to play our part. Guilt, shame, remorse and regret haunt our lives, and much of our effort is expended on avoiding them. We live in the eyes of judgement, and those eyes are also our own. From this springs the great longing in the human heart for righteousness, for the blameless life, the life that is properly guided. Being rightly guided, by the light that shines from

---

15. G. E. M. Anscombe, *Intention*, Oxford, Blackwell, 1957.

beyond the stars – such is the promise of salvation, according to Al-Ghazzali and the Sufi poets.

Some people feel this longing for purity more strongly than others. There are heroes of guilt, like Al-Ghazzali, Kierkegaard and St Thérèse de Lisieux, for whom the burden defines the direction of their lives. There are great artists – Dostoevsky, Dante, Botticelli and Wagner among them – who have made the search for purity into their dominant theme. And there are the ordinary, complacent people like you and me, for whom the quest for purity is an irritation, something to be got out of the way through some convenient ritual in which we can, for a blessed moment, own up to our condition and let the light shine in. Yet all of us, whatever our spiritual laxity, experience the constant need to refresh ourselves, to be purged of our transgressions, and to begin again with a clean slate. And this need for purity lies at the root of the religious urge. It is, quite simply, the price we pay for consciousness, the acknowledgement of the omnipresent 'why?'.[16] It is our recognition of the guilt that comes, from daring to exist as an 'I': what Schopenhauer aptly called *das Schuld des Daseins*.

Although I have been talking of three little words and the grammar of the personal pronoun, it should not have escaped the reader that I have also been discussing freedom. It was Kant who first made clear what I have been covertly assuming, which is that freewill enters our world through the 'I'. Contained within the first person perspective is a posture that distinguishes persons from all other things in nature, namely the ability to make themselves accountable for something that has not yet occurred. I *will* lift that stone, storm that fortress, kiss that woman. Saying such things I change my whole stance to the world, put myself in a condition of readiness, and do so by my own free choice.

16. For related thoughts see Vladimir Jankélévitch, *Le pur et l'impur*, Paris, Flammarion, 1960.

Every utterance, every train of thought, proceeds by these free gestures. And to that argument Kant added another, and for him far more powerful, consideration, namely that reason tells me not only to do certain things, but that I *ought* to do them. I ought to help that person in distress: and not doing so it is again *myself* that I blame. I focus on that very centre of being from which decisions flow the full force of moral condemnation. Our whole way of thinking about ourselves is built upon the 'moral law', and since 'ought' implies 'can', we can engage in practical reasoning only on the assumption that we are free.

But this leads to a strange question: what kind of world contains a thing like me – a thing with freedom and self-knowledge? It must be a world of enduring objects, Kant argued, objects with identity through time. And I am such an object: the thing which, deciding this here now, will do that there then. A world of enduring things is a world bound by causal laws: so Kant set out to prove in the immensely difficult section of the *Critique of Pure Reason* entitled 'The Transcendental Deduction of the Categories'. Without the web of causality, nothing 'preserves itself in being' long enough to know or be known. So my world, the world of the free being, is a world ordered by causal laws. And causal laws, Kant thought, are universal and necessary. They refer to connections in the very nature of things, connections that cannot be suspended on this or that occasion and merely for the convenience of people.

Building his argument in this way – by steps too many, too complex and too controversial to detain us here – Kant drew the following conclusion. Any being who can say 'I' and mean it is free; and any being who can say 'I' and mean it is situated in a world of universally binding causal laws. I am governed by a law of freedom, which compels my actions, and a law of nature, which binds me in the web of organic life. I am a free subject and a determined object: but I am not *two* things, a determined body with a free soul rattling inside.

I am *one* thing, which can be seen in two ways – as subject and as object. This is something that I know to be true, but which lies beyond understanding. I can never know *how* it is possible, only *that* it is possible.

That is a drastic way of putting something that I will try to put more gently as my argument proceeds. But it usefully brings us face to face once again with the scientific worldview, and in particular with the new way of describing human beings that has emerged from evolutionary psychology and neuroscience. Philosophers like Patricia Churchland and Daniel Dennett begin from the position I touched on at the beginning of this chapter, telling us that we human beings are to be understood as members of a particular species of ape, that our states of mind are rooted in adaptations formed during the long pre-historical period of the hunter-gatherer tribe, and that these adaptations are 'hard-wired in the human brain', as Churchland puts it.[17] If we want to know what kind of thing we are, therefore, how we are motivated and fulfilled and what we can cogently hope for, it is the brain we should be studying, not the mysterious thing called 'I', which word is, after all, not a name or a description but simply a context-dependent indexical term.

If we take this attitude, what remains of free will? In a well-known series of experiments, Benjamin Libet has used first electroencephalography and subsequently magnetic resonance imaging to explore the causal antecedents of human choice.[18] His results show that when people choose between alternatives, there is a particular burst of activity in the motor-centres of the brain leading directly to the action. But

17. See Patricia Churchland, *Neurophilosophy: Towards a Unified Science of the Mind-Brain*, Cambridge, Mass., MIT Press, 1986.
18. Libet's results and the conclusions he draws are summarized in his contribution to Robert Kane (ed.), *The Oxford Companion to Free Will*, Oxford, OUP, 2002. Kane brings together in masterly fashion all the arguments and positions that are most commonly defended now by analytical philosophers.

the subject himself reports his decision always some moments after this, when the action is already (from the point of view of the central nervous system) 'under way'. Some cognitive scientists (though not Libet) draw the conclusion that our impression of free choice is therefore an illusion, since 'choice' comes always too late, after the action has been set in motion by the brain. Some draw the further conclusion that it is the brain, not the person, that does everything, and that talk of persons and their actions is simply a loose and ignorant way of describing what should really be described in terms of a brain and the body that it moves.

Imagine two people discussing what to do: Jane wants to do X, Bill gives her reasons for doing Y, and these reasons change her mind. When does the decision occur? Surely when the reasons have been accepted, and when *that* is depends upon the pace of the dialogue. I could not engage in reasoning of this kind, if I did not assume that it was in my power to change my mind: nor could you. Freedom does not reside in some event that 'erupts' into consciousness unheralded by changes in the nervous system. It resides in practical reasoning, which is in turn founded in the relationality of the human person – the fact that people depend on each other for advice, are accountable for what they do, and are the objects of praise and blame.

The conclusion often drawn from Libet's experiment is that it shows any such picture to be confused. The 'brain', it is said, decides what to do, and our consciousness follows only later, when the switch has already been flipped. But this way of interpreting Libet's experiment assumes that an event in a *brain* is identical with a decision of a *person*,[19] that an action

---

19. This assumption is an instance of what Max Bennett and Peter Hacker have condemned as the 'mereological fallacy', the fallacy of explaining a property of a whole by attributing the same property to one of its parts. See *The Philosophical Foundations of Neuroscience*, Oxford, Blackwell, 2002, Part I, Chapter 3. Bennett and Hacker have their own reasons for rejecting the common interpretation of Libet's experiment: see *ibid.*, pp. 228–31.

is voluntary if and only if preceded by a mental episode of the right kind, that intentions and volitions are 'felt' episodes of a subject which can be precisely dated in time. All those assumptions are false. Sometimes an intentional action is preceded by a decision or choice, certainly; but usually the action *is* the choice. And what makes it intentional is not that it arose in a particular way but that the subject can say on no basis that *I* did this, or am doing this, and in saying so make himself accountable for it. To say that we are free is to point to this fact: namely that we can justify and criticize our actions, lay claim to them as our own, and know immediately and with certainty what we will do – not by predicting what we will do but by deciding to do it.

The Libet experiment leads to the denial of free will only if we also assume free choice to be an eruption in the stream of neural events. But to see freewill in that way is to look for it in the world of objects and not in the point of view of the subject, where it belongs. The same fallacy is committed by those who look for freedom in quantum effects, believing a free act to be one that originates in the quarks and leptons of the brain, at the sub-atomic level where nothing is rigidly determined. But to argue in that way is to construe the freedom of subjects as a kind of indeterminacy in objects – as a break in the chain of causality, so to speak, where the will can intervene. But freedom is not a kind of causality, still less an interruption of the causal order. Freedom emerges from the web of inter-personal relations, and comes into being as a corollary of 'I', 'you' and 'why?'. It is not a blip among objects but a revelation of the subject.

Some philosophers respond to such thoughts by dismissing the concept of freedom as folk psychology – part of that primitive science of the mind embedded in ordinary language, which neuroscience will one day replace.[20] But imagine what it

---

20. Thus Patricia Churchland in *Neurophilosophy*, *op. cit.*, though not Daniel C. Dennett in *Freedom Evolves*, New York, Viking Press, 2003.

would be like to replace our ordinary ways of understanding
human action with the theories of some future neuroscience.
Suppose I wonder why you have been avoiding me. I ask you
a direct question, and you accuse me of betraying your confi-
dences to a rival. I deny the charge, knowing it to be false, and
ask you why you think it to be true. You recount the evidence
and I refute it; your hostility disappears and we agree to work
together to limit the damage. That kind of dialogue occurs all
the time, and it is the way in which rational beings establish
and build on their relations. It presupposes at every point
that you and I both understand and make use of concepts
like belief and desire. And it assumes that we each have *first
person knowledge* of our beliefs and desires – that we don't
have to find out what they are but can summon them immediately and without evidence in response to the questions
'why?' and 'what?'. Use of the first person pronoun confers
the ability to describe immediately, on no basis, and with a
far-reaching immunity to certain kinds of error, the content of
one's present mental state, and also to put oneself forward as
accountable for one's deeds.

Suppose we now replace folk psychology with some explanatory neuroscience. The result would inevitably undermine
the use of our three metaphysical words. We would all be
condemned to a third-person view of ourselves and others: a
view of ourselves and others as objects. Each person would
become a 'he' or a 'she', and no I or you would remain. We
would be able to describe our mental condition only by
investigating our brains, and the give and take of reasons
between me and you would, since it depends on first person
privilege, disappear. With it would disappear the possibility
of inter-personal relations, and with inter-personal relations
would disappear language and all that has been built on it. In
short the neuroscience would be left with nothing of interest
to explain. That is just one thought among many tending
to the conclusion that our way of representing the human

world is not replaceable by neuroscience – not even by the neuroscience that explains our way of representing the human world.

An interesting corollary should be drawn from that sceptical position. You might say of Libet's experiments that they attempt to discover the place of the subject in the world of objects. They are looking for the point of intersection of the free self-consciousness with the world in which it acts. And they do not find that point. All that they find is a succession of events in the stream of objects, none of which can be identified with a free self-conscious choice. There is a parallel here with the question that I raised in the first chapter: the question of God's presence in the world. If you look on the world with the eyes of science it is impossible to find the place, the time, or the particular sequence of events that can be interpreted as showing God's presence. God disappears from the world, as soon as we address it with the 'why?' of explanation, just as the human person disappears from the world, when we look for the neurological explanation of his acts. So maybe God is a person like us, whose identity and will are bound up with his nature as a subject. Maybe we shall find him in the world where we are only if we cease to invoke him with the 'why?' of cause, and address him with the 'why?' of reason instead. And the 'why?' of reason must be addressed from I to you. The God of the philosophers disappeared behind the world, because he was described in the third person, and not addressed in the second.

The human world, I maintain, is ordered by concepts that are rooted in dialogue, and therefore in the first person perspective. But that perspective will not feature in the data of any science. There is no room in causal theories for terms like 'I' and 'you', and it is precisely this that gives rise to the revulsion that we feel – or at any rate, ought to feel – when a philosopher 'explains' human love, desire, longing, grief and resentment in terms like these:

The brains of social animals are wired to feel pleasure in the exercise of social dispositions such as grooming and cooperation, and to feel pain when shunned, scolded, or excluded. Neurochemicals such as vasopressin and oxytocin mediate pair-bonding, parent-offspring bonding, and probably also bonding to kith and kin ... [21]

Those remarks are from Patricia Churchland, and typify a current of philosophical thinking that has gathered strength in the wake of her call for a 'neurophilosophy'. In response I should say that the *brains* of social animals feel neither pleasure nor pain. Pleasure and pain are what *we* feel, and we are not identical with our brains. And I reject the reduction of 'I–You' relationships to forms of bonding that require neither first person awareness nor even consciousness for their achievement. If this is what it is, to replace 'folk psychology' by 'neuroscience', then we should protest that neuroscience purchases its explanations at the cost of the facts. Indeed, we are not dealing with a new science of the human being at all, but with an outpouring of neurononsense.

This nonsense comes about because people can be conceptualized in two ways: as organisms and as objects of personal interaction. The first way employs the concept 'human being' (a natural kind); it divides our actions at the joints of explanation, and derives our behaviour from a biological science of man. The second way employs the concept 'person', which is not the concept of a natural kind, but *sui generis*.[22] Through this concept, and the associated notions of freedom, responsi-

21. Patricia Churchland, 'Human Dignity from a Neurophilosophical Perspective', in *Human Dignity and Bioethics*, essays commissioned by the President's Council on Bioethics, Washington, 2008, p. 103. For a comprehensive attack on this kind of thinking see Raymond Tallis, *Aping Mankind: Neuromania, Darwinitis and the Misrepresentation of Humanity*, Durham, Acumen, 2011.
22. See Robert Spaemann, *Persons: The Difference between 'Someone' and 'Something'*, trans. Oliver O'Donovan, Oxford, OUP, 2006.

bility, reason for action, right, duty, justice and guilt, we gain the description under which a human being is seen, by those who respond to him or her as a person. It is a description of a creature that sees itself as both free and fallen, a creature with a legacy of religious need. And when people endeavour to understand this creature through the half-formed theories of neuroscience they are tempted to pass over its distinctive features in silence, or else to attribute them to some brain-shaped homunculus inside.

This is not the place to raise the question of the relation between people and their brains – a question that has been the subject of Gifford Lectures by two of the great pioneers of modern neuroscience: *Man on His Nature*, 1936/7 by Sir Charles Sherrington, and *The Human Mystery*, 1977/8, by Sir John Eccles. Both of those writers believed that we will solve the mystery of consciousness by finding the point of interaction between mind and brain. But neither saw that the 'mystery' to which they referred arose from the privileged view of the subject, and lies on the horizon within which the world of the subject plays itself out. We can see this from a well-known thought experiment of Hilary Putnam's, which has its counterpart in the popular film *The Matrix*.[23] Putnam imagines a brain kept in a vat of nutrients and stimulated by a controlling scientist so as to produce exactly the neural activity of a normal human being in a normal life. Putnam's example is a reconstruction of Descartes' sceptical argument about dreaming, and prompts the question: how do I know that *I* am not such a brain?

If we reflect a little further on the case, however, we must surely conclude that, if 'I' thoughts are engendered by this

23. *Reason, Truth and History*, Cambridge, Mass., MIT Press, 1981. See also Robert Nozick's development of a comparable thought experiment in *Philosophical Explanations*, Oxford, OUP, 1981, Chapter 3, and the discussion of this by J. J. Valberg, *Dream, Death and the Self*, *op. cit.*, pp. 114–17.

process, they do not occur in this brain at all. The subject of these 'experiences' is not even in the same space as the brain that supposedly gives rise to them. He lives in a space of his own, the space of a human life in which he moves and feels and thinks. He must, if his experience is to be both real and metaphysically possible, inhabit a world of other people, who can identify him through his body and engage with him in dialogue. And his body in that space will contain a brain – the brain that is truly his, that belongs to the person he identifies when he says, speaking in the first person, 'I am here'. The brain that the scientist stimulates has no connection, not even a causal connection, with the brain of the person he supposedly controls, since there is no space–time continuum that contains them both.

One conclusion to draw is that Putnam's thought experiment is incoherent. A more important conclusion is that no attempt to pin down the subject in the world of objects will ever really succeed. You can extract from the person as many body parts as you will, but you will never find the place where he is, the place from which he addresses me and which I in turn address. What matters to us are not the invisible nervous systems that explain how people work, but the visible appearances to which we respond when we respond to them as people. It is these appearances that we interpret, and upon our interpretation we build responses that must in turn be interpreted by those to whom they are directed. It seems, then, that there is an impassable metaphysical gap, between the human object and the free subject to whom we relate as a person. The very difficulty that we encounter in our relation to the God of the philosophers stands in the way of our relation to each other. Yet we constantly cross that seemingly impassable metaphysical barrier. How is this? And if we can understand how it is, will that help us to solve the problem of the relation between the transcendental and the immanent God?

To summarize: You can situate human beings entirely in the world of objects. In doing so you will in all probability reduce them to animals whose behaviour is to be explained by some combination of evolutionary psychology and neuroscience. But then you will find yourself describing a world from which human action, intention, responsibility, freedom and emotion have been wiped away: it will be a world without a face. The face shines in the world of objects with a light that is *not* of this world – the light of subjectivity. You can look for freedom in the world of objects and you will not find it: not because it is not there, but because it is bound up with the first person perspective, and with the view from somewhere of the creature who can say 'I'.

3

Where Am I?

The god whose doings are recounted in the Torah does not, at first sight, look very much like the god of the philosophers. Yet, in his own way, he is hidden and, despite his busy and all-encompassing interest in worldly affairs, he acts at a distance from his devotees. In Exod. 33.20 God says to Moses 'Thou canst not see my face, for there shall no man see me and live' – although Moses is permitted a rear view of the Lord, as he passes by. The imagery throughout the book of Exodus is strange and disturbing: God stands proxy for all that we do not know and cannot control, for all the areas of life in which we might unknowingly step on ground that gives way beneath us to our ruin. He is nowhere and everywhere, lying in wait for us and also fleeing as soon as he is sensed.[1]

Yet there is one thing that God says about himself which is of universal significance, and this he says on his first encounter with Moses, speaking from the burning bush. Moses seeks to know the name of God, in order that he can testify to the authenticity of his vision. But God refuses to name himself, saying instead 'I am that I am'; adding that, if the Israelites

1. See, in this connection, Jack Miles's riveting deconstruction: *God: A Biography*, New York, Alfred A. Knopf, 1996.

ask for some guarantee of his mission, Moses is to say that he has been sent by 'I AM'.[2] Everything else about God is accidental; this alone is essential: that he refers to himself in the first person. In other words he, like us, is a person, who can utter the word 'I' and relate to his worshippers I to you. He is to be addressed as another subject. Hence he reaches out to his people not through coercion and force, but through a covenant – in other words, a mutual agreement, in which he makes himself accountable to those who accept his terms.

Talmudic authorities regard the Torah (the first five books of the Old Testament) as a record of revelations granted to Moses and first set down by him. Modern biblical scholarship regards the Torah rather as a compilation, put together during the Babylonian exile from four or more earlier sources. However you look at it this document contains, in narrative and imagistic form, profound truths about God's relation to the world, expressed in a way that immediately engages the emotions of the reader. God is a person, an agent, and an 'I'. And he relates to his people through promises, obligations, laws and covenants – all of which presuppose that both he and they are free agents, able to change the flow of events, and at the same time to take responsibility for doing so. In this chapter I want to say something about what that involves. In particular I want to raise the question: what and where am I, in the world of objects? That question, I maintain, is a necessary preliminary to the question of God's presence: the question what, and where, is God? The question of God's presence often looks insoluble. Rightly understood, however, it resembles the question of your and my presence. And we must try to answer them both together.

2. Hebrew (like other Semitic languages) has only a partially defined present-tense for the verb 'to be'; hence the words that I have given in the King James translation are in the future tense in the original. But it is their first person grammar that God is emphasizing.

The Torah constantly returns to the paradox of the transcendental God who is immanent in the world of his creation. God is shown as 'moving among' the Israelites. He is a real presence (*shekhinah*) in their midst, and his covenant requires not merely that they obey his laws, but that they erect a house for him, a place in which he can be encountered (even if never 'face to face'). But God's emphasis on ritual, cleanliness, and the punctilious arrangements for housing him, which are supposedly the conditions of his presence, also emphasize his absence. The temple is God's point of entry into this world, the 'point of intersection of the timeless with time', to borrow Eliot's words. It is the place of a God who acts in this world, while being impassably removed from it. The ritual is designed to show this – to keep the people at a distance from the Holy of Holies, shut off from God by everything except their obedience. The paradox of the transcendent God who is immanent in the world of his creation, of the eternal and immutable who moves and changes in time, of the remote sustainer who is an object and subject of love – this paradox is symbolized in the rituals of the temple and also resolved there. Do we just say that these are things we cannot understand, and that the ritual is there to rescue the incomprehensible by re-presenting it as a mystery? That is often said of the Christian Eucharist. But it makes the dividing line between faith and scepticism too fine.

Let us look again at God's response to the question posed by Moses. Moses asked for God's name: in other words for an *identification* – something that would enable Moses to know who it is that he is talking to. And God responds by identifying himself in the first person. He is saying to Moses that he, God, is a self-conscious subject. Like Moses, God has a subjective point of view. He does not exist only outside the world, with a view from nowhere that he can never share. He moves in the world, in a somewhere of his own.

This is a radical thing for the *causa sui* to claim. It is precisely what sends shivers down the Islamic spine. How can God be greater than everything, a transcendental unity without parts or partners, if he is also in the world, addressing his creatures in the first person case? Sure, he occasionally lapses into the first person (usually the first person plural) in the Koran: but only in ways that make it clear that it is really the other, and not the self, that is speaking. He speaks *through* the angel Gabriel, and *through* the recitations of the Prophet – which is what the word 'qur'ân' (recital) implies. But he is not an 'I' among others in a world that he shares. The unity of God, in Islamic thought, is not simply a matter of God's being the unique instance of something: it is a metaphysical condition that nothing else can manifest. Spinoza took this thought seriously, arguing that there is at least one *causa sui* and also at most one. Hence everything that exists is a mode of the one substance, and there is no distinction between God and the world. I find it hard to believe that the Islamic doctrine of *tawHîd* can avoid moving in the same direction. If we do go in this direction, however, God's presence becomes an *ubiquitous* presence, in which we are all absorbed, and none of us relates to God as Moses thought he did, I to you and you to me.

Obviously, we need to get a little clearer about the meaning of the word 'I'. Philosophers have frequently argued that 'I' does not function as a name, and does not provide an identifying description of the speaker. Moreover, when I refer to myself in the first person I do not apply some criterion of identity, some method or procedure that enables me to say 'this thing, to which I am referring, is I'. If I used such a procedure, then I could misapply it: I could make mistakes, coming to the conclusion that this thing that I am referring to is not I but someone or something else. And that supposition is absurd.

This does not mean that the word 'I' is empty. 'I' is an indexical term, like 'here' and 'now'; but it is also (although some philosophers have doubted this[3]) a referring expression, correctly used only of a certain kind of thing – namely of a self-conscious and self-referring subject. Moreover the word 'I' can be meaningfully replaced in all its occurrences by other pronouns or by a proper name. 'I am Roger Scruton' is a statement of identity, and one about which I could be wrong, even though I make it with special authority, having had a lifelong acquaintance with Roger Scruton.

When speaking in the first person I can refer authoritatively to an object in the external world. I know, for example, that I am sitting down at a desk, and from this I infer that a particular body – namely my body – is disposed in a particular way. When I move my arm I know immediately and on no basis that my arm has moved, and any error in this matter must be explained in some special way. I may see an arm in a mirror and wonder whether it is mine; but in all normal perceptions I have an immediate awareness of my body and can identify it without criteria as mine.

Likewise, when I attribute mental states to myself there is, over a large range of cases, both immediate awareness and also a kind of immunity to error. I know that I have a pain in my finger, that I am thinking of Sam, and that I am hungry. And I know on no basis, and without deploying a criterion of identity, that this pain, this thought and this hunger belong to *one* thing, which is *I*. Of course, I could be wrong in thinking that this I is Roger Scruton: I might in fact be Gordon Brown, suffering from delusions of grandeur. But I cannot be wrong in thinking that this unity that I identify is I. This recalls Kant's 'transcendental unity of apperception'. A self-conscious being, Kant argued, apprehends the unity of the I, and this unity

3. See, for example, G. E. M. Anscombe, 'The First Person', in *Collected Papers*, Oxford, Blackwell, 1981, vol. 2. The peculiarities of the first person case are not to be explained by saying that 'I' does not refer, but by specifying *how* the word 'I' refers. See Christopher Peacocke, 'The First Person as a Case Study', Chapter 3 of *Truly Understood*, Oxford, OUP, 2008.

is transcendental in that it is not something that the subject arrives at by way of a conclusion, but something presupposed in all his knowledge, including the knowledge that he has of himself.

So here is what God is saying to Moses: I am *one* thing, with the kind of unity that you discover in yourself, when you are alert and addressing another. This transcendental unity does not tell you to what kind you belong, or what role you have in the world of objects: it identifies you, rather, as a unique point of view *upon* the world of objects. And in that respect, God is saying, he is like us. He has that 'transcendental' and 'original' uniqueness which is implied by his mastery of the first person case. More, he can know himself as *one* without implying that there are others like him in any other respect. Maybe there is more to his unity than this – maybe he is 'simple' and 'substantial' as the medieval philosophers thought; maybe he has that ineffable *tawHîd* that the Muslims so fervently believe in. But what is interesting to me is that he is claiming to be present in our world in something like the way that we are present: through a view from somewhere that grants him a place as a subject in the world of things.

I can know myself as I only if I can spontaneously refer to myself, identify my mental states, situate myself in relation to others. All of those capacities involve mental acts that depend upon a shared public language. I must understand 'I' as a pronoun that others can use, which retains its sense as the speaker (and therefore the reference) changes, and which can be replaced by other pronouns without the resulting sentence ceasing to be syntactically well-formed. I am I to myself only if I am also you to others, and this means that I must be capable of that free dialogue in which I take charge of my presence before the presence of you. The same, surely, has to be true of God, if Moses is to encounter him.

You may wonder *how* God can be free to act, in a world in which everything is governed by scientific laws. You may think that the relation of dependence, which binds the world as a whole to the necessary being, leaves science in charge, when it comes to saying what causes what. And science cannot, in the nature of things, trace an empirical event to a transcendental cause. But there is a way out of that objection – or at least, a way of postponing the answer to it. As I argued in the last chapter, the human being is situated in the world of objects, and is himself an object in that world. All attempts to pin-point his freedom and agency in the world of objects will lead to the kind of nonsense that we find in Libet's account of the neuroscience of decision. Look for God's will in the physical world and you will certainly find it, just as you will find my will in the world in which I move. But look for the 'gap' in the physical order, the inexplicable departure from the laws of nature, which is the physical 'reality' of God's will, and you will find nothing. Freedom, action and accountability are properties of the person, and it is only when we see God as a person that we will under-stand that this is true also of him. He is present in our world in the same sense that we are: as a subject. And when we attribute an event to his will, we are saying that there is a reason for it, and that this reason is God's answer to our own question 'why?'. We are not describing it as a miraculous intervention, and we can accept Hume's scepticism about miracles, while acknowledging God's presence as an agent in space and time.

This does not mean that there is no puzzle about God's agency: of course there is. But it is a special case of the puzzle about agency *as such*. What is it, to *act* in the world, and how is the capacity for action connected with the first person point of view? Clearly, it would be a mistake to approach this question by starting from the problem of God's agency, which is a limiting case. We need to begin from our own position, and ask how it is that we act in the world, and what makes action possible.

The first thing to note is that persons are not only subjects: they are objects among others in a world that they share. They are living, breathing, acting beings, embodied and occupying physical space. Moreover, they are not *two* things: a human body and a soul inside. To think in that Cartesian way is to 'reify' the subject – in other words to commit the error that Kant identified, in the Paralogisms chapter of the *Critique of Pure Reason*. This is the error of supposing that the subject can be understood as objects are understood, through categories of substance and cause. The subject is the view from somewhere, but does not appear within that view: for if it did so I might misidentify it, or even conclude that there is no such thing.

It is just as possible to develop a science of the human being as it is to develop a science of any other animal. The theory of evolution and the science of the brain promise to show what makes this peculiar organism 'tick': and maybe it will turn out to be not so very different from what makes other organisms tick – in particular those organisms that are close to us on the evolutionary tree. If we deny that, then we deny the best explanations so far given of man's place in nature. Creationists think they have a better explanation: but that is because they fail to see that they have no explanation at all, but merely a formula for translating the unexplained into the inexplicable.

At the same time we are presented with a problem, when it comes to accounting for our ways of understanding and relating to each other: for we don't relate to each other as animals, not even when doing the things – fighting, grooming, copulating – that dominate the social lives of animals. We see each other as the originators of our acts: the person comes before us as a thing that *enters the world through his actions*. The causal chains that bind past to future run through us as they run through everything. But we do not refer our thoughts, actions and emotions to their endless prelude in the world of objects, but to the subject who accounts for them, and within whose first person perspective they lie. Hence we make, or ought to make, a metaphysical distinction between the acts of humans and the doings of animals. It is true that animals have beliefs and desires as we do, and that their wants, needs and feelings cause their behaviour. But they are not revealed in their behaviour as we are in ours. They do not 'intervene' in the world as we do: they do not take charge of the future or make themselves accountable for it. The person is revealed as an individual in his actions, and for this reason there exists in all natural languages the idiom of 'agent causation', as it has been called.[4] We refer to actions as events; but we identify their causes not as events but as agents. It is not the movement of John's arm that caused Mary to fall, but John, who pushed her. John is the cause of all those things that immediately issue from his will.

Moreover, while we all belong to a natural kind – being members of the species *homo sapiens* – it is not as members of that kind that we identify ourselves, when we refer to ourselves in the first person. We identify ourselves as persons, and assume that we endure as persons. As a human being I have a past and a future; as a person I lay claim to that past and that future as mine – as things that originate in me, in this very subject who must account for them. Persons do not form a natural kind, and the concept of personal identity is problematic in a way that the concept of animal identity is not. This we have surely learned from countless thought experiments, from John Locke to Sydney Shoemaker and Derek Parfit.[5]

Other animals are conscious: which is to say that they respond to their environment by responding to how it *seems*.

---

4. See Timothy O'Connor, *Persons and Causes*, Oxford, OUP, 2002.
5. Sydney Shoemaker, *Self-Knowledge and Self-Identity*, Ithaca, Cornell University Press, 1963; Derek Parfit, *Reasons and Persons*, Oxford, Clarendon Press, 1984.

Animals are repositories of 'seemings', and this lifts them, to a certain extent, from the world of objects and sets them nearer to ourselves. We can relate to them not by pushing them around, as we relate to ordinary physical things, but by changing the way things seem to them. We offer rewards and punishments; we address them with shouts and murmurs; we stroke them, feed them and get them to see the world in a way that makes them pliable to our interests – including our interest in their well-being.

But consciousness is not the same as self-consciousness. It involves sensitivity to information, an ability to respond to stimuli, and a repertoire of needs and desires. But it does not involve the crucial thing that God claimed in addressing Moses – the ability not merely to have mental states, but to attribute them to a centre of consciousness, and to identify that centre of consciousness in the first person, as a person like you. Anthropomorphism does not consist in attributing mental states to animals, or in imagining them to be thinking and feeling as we think and feel. It involves seeing them as persons, who identify themselves in the first person, and divide the world into 'I' and 'not-I', self and other, me and you. To think of animals in that way is to suppose that they, like we, have the 'point of view of the subject', that they, like we, address the world of objects from a place at its edge. And that is to assume something for which we have, and could have, no grounds.[6]

This division between I and not-I, which Fichte rightly saw as the distinguishing feature of the rational intellect, lies also at the root of the moral life. For with the idea of the self comes that of the other – of the other who is another like me. *That* is what God was pointing out to Moses, and what the Jewish revelation has transmitted down the centuries – that

6. Arguments around this issue are endless, tedious and full of undigested venom. I have outlined my own position in *Animal Rights and Wrongs*, London, Continuum, 2003.

the free being, who can say 'I', must acknowledge the equal existence of the other. It is why the original commandment, to love God entirely, contains the second, to love your neighbour as yourself.

This takes us back to a point that I dwelt on in the previous chapter, which is that of the essential relationality of the person. Persons are the kind of thing that can recognize others as persons and be recognized in turn as persons.[7] Persons are accountable to others, and see themselves as others in the eyes of others. They enter the world of objects as 'things to be judged', and are therefore encumbered by duties and gifted with rights. This point goes radically against the fashionable, but to my mind nonsensical, habit of seeing moral problems in utilitarian terms, as problems that we solve by a kind of economic calculus. Real morality begins where economics stops: at the threshold of the other. Through the ideas of right and duty we set the ground rules for a negotiated life among strangers. These rules tell us that rights are to be respected, and duties obeyed. They confer equality of moral status on all participants to the moral dialogue, and impose on us an obligation to justify our conduct in the face of adverse criticism. They bring with them a battery of concepts that entirely transform the worldview and emotions of those who possess them: concepts like justice, desert and punishment, which lie at the heart of our inter-personal responses.

Because they must think in that way, self-conscious subjects enter the world of objects already equipped for tragedy. They know that they are judged, just as they judge. They know they must account for their actions, and that mistakes and defects will be laid at their door. They feel shame – the *Schutzgefühl* as Max Scheler describes it, which protects them from adverse

---

7. For the development of this idea, see Robert Spaemann: *Persons: The Difference Between 'Someone' and 'Something'*, trans. Oliver O'Donovan, Oxford, OUP, 2007.

judgement[8] – and guilt, the self-punishment that comes from the consciousness of wrong. The original sin is not one committed by their distant ancestors in the Garden of Eden. It is, to repeat Schopenhauer's words, *das Schuld des Daseins* – the guilt of existence itself, existence as a someone.

There is another and yet more puzzling feature of the concept of the person that we need to notice. Persons are not just particulars: they are individuals. We distinguish them and count them, as we do the animals. But they also have, or seem to have, a robust identity through time of which they themselves are the producers. Derek Parfit and others have tried to replace the concept of personal identity with that of the momentary self. But there can be no such thing as a momentary self. Being a *self* is not just a matter of consciousness: it is a matter of taking responsibility for one's acts and passions, of recognizing the long beams cast into past and future by the 'I' that shines in the now. I can act in the present only if I take responsibility for the future, and this means that I must recognize my identity as a person through time. Any attempt to dispense with identity through time amounts merely to empty scepticism of the kind expressed by Hume, who was sceptical about personal identity for the reason that he was sceptical about all statements of identity, namely, that they involve claims about other times than now. That scepticism is too general to distinguish a special problem about personal identity, and it surprises me that its application by Parfit and others has been received as anything more than a game.

Nevertheless, the concept of personal identity creates a striking philosophical problem. Personhood is not a *property* that I possess, but my way of being me. I am a person only because there is a *compromised individual* who I am. In the

8. Max Scheler, *Über Scham und Schamgefühl*, 1913, in *Gesammelte Werke*, Bd. 10, Berne, Francke, 1957.

world of objects there is the animal, the member of the species *homo sapiens*, which you can single out as you single out any other individual thing. But in *my* world, the world of the subject, there seems to be something else, not a 'reidentifiable particular', but a free individual, whose identity through time is his own responsibility and in some sense his own creation. Somehow the human animal in the world of objects is identical with the person who I am: but how, under what sortal, and with what criterion of identity? There are those who follow Locke, arguing for personal identity as 'the continuity of consciousness', and believing that, in some way, the self-revelation of the subject in memory and intention establishes another kind of durability from that of the embodied human being. Locke's argument was famously accused of circularity by Bishop Butler. More interesting, from my point of view, is the fact that it repeats the error diagnosed by Kant – the error of situating the subject in the world of objects as one object among others.[9] Just as we search the world of objects in vain for the place where freedom enters, so do we search it in vain for the self. Yet selves are also persons, who exist and act in that world, which is the only world that we have. How is this possible?

The paradox can be softened through a concept that has played a large part in post-Kantian philosophy, and which has been a constant theme of modern art and literature – the concept of self-realization. Through our actions we do not merely express our states of mind and intentions: we make ourselves present in the world. And in the course of doing this

9. See the discussion by David Wiggins in *Sameness and Substance Renewed*, Cambridge, CUP, 2001, Chapter 7. Wiggins sides with Butler against Locke, but argues in opposition to Butler's immaterialism that our identity through time is governed not by 'same person' but by 'same human being'. A comparable position is taken, in the face of all the crazy thought experiments, some conjured by himself, by Mark Johnston, in *Surviving Death*, Princeton, Princeton University Press, 2011.

we also change. What we are for ourselves minutely reflects what we are for others, since it is through our dialogue with others that we understand how we appear in the world. The I–You encounter shapes both me and you, and freedom should not be seen as the premise of this encounter but as its conclusion. By learning to see myself as you see me, I gain control of my situation, as a being in the world. And I learn what I am by imprinting myself on what I am not. Through the life of civil society, through religion, art and institutions, I shape myself as an other in the eyes of others, and so gain consciousness of myself as a subject who acts freely in a world that I share.

In a famous passage of *The Phenomenology of Spirit*[10] Hegel argues that I–You encounters, which begin in conflict and pass through a stage of subjection, intrinsically tend towards justice – towards the situation in which each party acknowledges the other's right to equal treatment, and in which relations are founded not on coercion but on consent. This is not the place to rehearse Hegel's complex argument. Suffice it to say that while we are persons by nature, this nature is realized or actualized in what we become. And Hegel shows, to my satisfaction at least, that the process of becoming fully individual and self-aware involves coming to see myself as others see me, as a 'you' in the world of others, as well as an 'I' in the world that is mine. Through our free actions we are present in the world as persons. But we can be present only because we are present to others, and that means present objectively, in human form. The identity of the person and the human being is therefore something that we achieve, by putting the 'I' on display in the visible 'he' or 'she'. This is the process that Fichte and Hegel call *Entäusserung*, the 'outward-forming' or objectification of the subject, who

10. *The Phenomenology of Spirit*, trans. A. Miller, Oxford, Clarendon Press, 1977, pp. 111–18.

comes to know himself in just this way. And it connects with what other thinkers have called 'positive freedom'.[11]

An analogy might help. When painters apply paint to canvas they create physical objects by purely physical means. Any such object is composed of areas and lines of paint, arranged on a surface that we can regard, for the sake of argument, as two-dimensional. When we look at the surface of the painting, we see those areas and lines of paint, and also the surface that contains them. But that is not all we see. We also see – for example – a face that looks out at us with smiling eyes. In one sense the face is a property of the canvas, over and above the blobs of paint; for you can observe the blobs and not see the face, and vice versa. And the face is really there: someone who does not see it is not seeing correctly. On the other hand, there is a sense in which the face is not an additional property of the canvas, over and above the lines and blobs. For as soon as the lines and blobs are there, so is the face. Nothing more needs to be added, in order to generate the face – and if nothing more needs to be added, the face is surely nothing more. Moreover, every process that produces just these blobs of paint, arranged in just this way, will produce just this face – even if the artist is unaware of the face. (Imagine how you would design a machine for producing Mona Lisas.)

The person emerges in the human being in something like that way. It is not something over and above the life and behaviour in which we observe it, but not reducible to them either. Once personhood has emerged it is possible to relate to a human being in a new way – the way of personal relations.

---

11. See Isaiah Berlin's classic essay on 'Two Concepts of Liberty', which is not, however, a defence of, so much as a warning against, the cult of self realization. See also, for influential applications of Hegel's argument to the basic forms of modern life, Alexandre Kojève, ed. Raymond Queneau, *Introduction à la lecture de Hegel*, Paris, Gallimard, 1947, and Ernst Bloch, 'Phänomenologie des Geistes' in *Subjekt-Objekt: Erläuterungen zu Hegel* (1951), second edn, Frankfurt am Main, Suhrkamp, 1962.

(In like manner we can relate to a picture in ways that we cannot relate to something that we see merely as a distribution of pigments.) With this new order of relation comes a new order of understanding, in which reasons and meanings, rather than causes, are sought in answer to the question 'why?': the order of the covenant. With persons we are in dialogue: we call upon them to justify their conduct in our eyes, as we must justify our conduct in theirs. Central to this dialogue are concepts of freedom, choice and accountability, and these concepts have no place in the description of animal behaviour, just as the concept of a human being has no place in the description of the physical make-up of a picture, even though it is a picture in which a human being can be seen.

That is only an analogy, however, and we should not think that it solves the deep metaphysical problems that have been occupying me. The face in the picture inhabits an imagined world; the person before me lives in the real world of space and time. I have been discussing the place of freedom in the world of causality, and the place of the subject in the world of objects. Language seems to fall silent at the threshold of these problematic notions: they lie at the limit, and can be grasped only by one further step that we cannot take, the step beyond the edge of the world. We know that the two problems – freedom and causality, subject and object – have a common structure, and that they must have a solution. But perhaps it is beyond the power of the human mind to find that solution.

A picture is a surface, which presents to the normal educated eye an aspect of a thing depicted. Pictures therefore form a functional kind: the kind of thing that presents an aspect to the self-conscious observer. Members of this kind include an enormous variety of objects: canvases, sheets of paper, computer screens, holographs, and so on. The functional kind subsumes things that belong to many different natural kinds.

Likewise persons are a kind – though not a natural kind. It is true that the behavioural complexity required to exemplify inter-personal responses, to entertain 'I'-thoughts, and to hold oneself and others accountable for changes in the world, is something that we witness only in members of a particular natural kind – the kind *homo sapiens*. But could we not envisage other beings, members of some other species or of no biological species at all, who exhibit the same complexity and are able to engage with us, I to I? If so, they belong with us in the order of things, and there is a kind that includes us both. I doubt that dolphins are like us in the relevant respects. To become like us they would have to live with each other *face to face*, and how is that possible for a creature without a face? In the cartoon films, however, animals *acquire* faces, by speaking from their mouths, addressing each other through their eyes, reshaping their heads to exhibit facial movements and self-conscious expressions, and claiming the voice that speaks from within them as the voice that is 'mine'. The same is true of the more plausibly 'personal' of the aliens that are conjured in science fiction films.

Return for a moment to the evolutionary theory of altruism. The soldier ant who marches vainly into the fire, under the genetic imperative to defend the ant-heap, is doing something that superficially resembles what the officer does, who throws himself on to a live grenade in order to protect his troops. The ant dies in the service of its genes. And the evolutionary psychologists would like to say something similar of the officer. But that is not true. He dies in the service of *others*. His motive is one of self-sacrifice, on behalf of his troops – a motive that is available only to a subject who distinguishes self and other, who has the concept of sacrifice, and who can make a *gift* of his life to another like himself. 'Greater love hath no man than this, that he lay down his life for his friend,' said Christ. The world of the self-conscious being is a world in which there is *love* as well as attachment, and in which others exist as objects of obligation, places in the web of objects where light streams in from another source. Hence it is a world in which just and unjust, virtuous and vicious, beautiful and ugly, right and wrong are all distinguished.

The example shows how the 'I' concept penetrates the human world. The world perceived from this perspective makes demands that no animal can recognize, and is arranged according to concepts and kinds that no animal can perceive. We should not be surprised, therefore, that our understanding of the human world cannot be captured by the science of objects. The self-conscious mind paints the world in the colours of subjectivity – and the result is in no way to be dismissed as an illusion, any more than the face in the picture is an illusion. For a long time philosophers have been aware of these facts, recognizing that self-conscious beings live in a world that is *to be interpreted*, and not merely *to be explained*. Unfortunately, those who have taken this distinction seriously, from Wilhelm Dilthey to Paul Ricoeur, have not always written clearly about the meanings that they allege to be so important to us.[12]

This brings me to another argument that might help to soften the paradoxes that I have been placing before the reader. I have argued that there is more than one meaning to the question 'why?' and that the 'why?' of science, which looks for causes, should be distinguished from the 'why' of reason, which looks for arguments, and the 'why?' of understanding, which looks for meanings. It is not only our enquiries that follow these separate paths; so too do our ways of ordering the world. Science attempts to divide nature at the joints, to group together those things that have a shared structure and a shared causal history. Its theories deploy concepts of natural kinds and primitive variables, and respect the surface phenomena only so far as is necessary to explain them. Things that we group together for our purposes, such as tables,

---

12. There is a by-way of the intellectual life here that I wish to avoid. The interested reader will see why by consulting the collection of Ricoeur's writings edited by John B. Thompson, *Paul Ricoeur: Hermeneutics and the Human Sciences*, Cambridge, CUP, 1981.

weapons and amusements, may have nothing in common from the point of view of science, while things which science groups together for the purpose of explanation, such as fungi, silicates, and electromagnetic waves, may have nothing significant in common from the point of view of human uses.

When describing the human world – the world as we interact with it – we frequently replace the 'why?' of explanation, which leads the scientist towards the fundamental structures of the world, with another question 'why?', turned back from the world towards our interests. We classify things under concepts of functional, moral and aesthetic kinds, and of kinds that are themselves changed by our concept of them, like the kind 'person' to which we belong.[13] These concepts inform our states of mind, and we perceive the world in terms of them. I look about me and see tables and chairs, ornaments and symbols. I read the world as a sign and an invitation, and the concepts that I use focus my emotions and interests on what is useful and meaningful to me. The fearful, the tragic, the amusing, the delightful: who is to say that these categories denote anything deep in the things to which they apply, rather than in the experience of the one who applies them? We distinguish just and unjust, comfortable and uncomfortable, shameful and respectable, just as we distinguish colours and patterns, without inquiring into the underlying motion that throws up these appearances in its wake.

Here is an example of what I have in mind: the concept of a melody. Every musical person can distinguish melodies from mere sequences of notes. Melodies have a beginning, a middle and an end; they begin and they continue until they stop; they have an individual identity and atmosphere, can be combined and developed according to their inner logic; they can be

---

13. Such 'interactive kinds' have been interestingly explored by Ian Hacking, 'The Looping Effect of Human Kinds', in Dan Sperber *et al.* (eds), *Causal Cognition: An Interdisciplinary Approach*, Oxford, OUP, 1995, pp. 351–83.

taken apart, amplified, augmented and diminished. They are the stuff of music and unless you can identify them you will be deaf to what music means. But no science of sound has use for the concept of a melody. As far as acoustics is concerned, melodies are sequences of pitched sounds like any other. Sequences that we hear as melodies are not a different kind of thing from sequences that we hear as meaningless successions, and phenomenal features like tension and release, forward motion, gravitational attraction and sounding through silence don't appear in acoustics. The concept of melody classifies sounds according to a highly sophisticated human interest, and that interest is an interest in surfaces and signs, not in the physical facts that underpin them.[14] Yet melodies are musical individuals, which endure through change, and can be identified as 'the same again'.

The example shows that there are concepts which direct our mental states but which can play no role in an explanatory theory, because they divide the world into the wrong kinds of kind – concepts like those of ornament, melody, duty, freedom. The concept of the person is such a concept, which does not mean that there are no persons, but only that a scientific theory of human persons will classify them with other things – for example, with apes or mammals – and will not be a scientific theory of every kind of person. (For example, it will not be a theory of corporate persons, of angels, or of God.) Hence the kind to which we belong is defined through a concept that does not feature in the science of human biology. Biology sees us as objects rather than subjects, and its descriptions of our responses are not descriptions of what we feel. The study of our *kind* is the business of the *Geisteswissenschaften,* which are not sciences at all, but 'humanities' – in other words, exercises in inter-personal understanding. I have in mind the

14. See Roger Scruton, *The Aesthetics of Music*, Oxford, OUP, 1997, Chapters 1 and 2.

kind of understanding exhibited when we explain why King Lear is a tragic figure, why 'smiling through tears' is an apt description of the Cavatina in Beethoven's B-flat quartet, why Rembrandt's self-portraits show death and decay as a personal possession, and all the other matters that form a true *éducation sentimentale*.

The kind-concept under which we assemble human beings influences our understanding of their psychological states. These are understood as the states of persons, and not as states that non-personal animals might equally exhibit. And the way we understand them influences the way we experience them. The example of sexual feelings provides a vivid illustration of what I mean. Sexual relations, the biologist might argue, are to be explained in terms of genetic strategies. There is no difficulty in accounting for phenomena like jealousy, female modesty, male predatoriness, and the well-known typologies of attraction, once we see these things as aspects of genetic 'investment'. My response to this is to say: that is fine, so far as it goes. But the explanations given under-determine the behaviour to be explained. The feature that most needs explaining is precisely the inter-personal intentionality that distinguishes us from our evolutionary neighbours, and causes our attachments to 'reach through' the empirical circumstances that give rise to them towards the free subject who is their target. Sexual jealousy in a person is not like its simulacrum in a bonobo, since it involves the thought of betrayal, for which another person is answerable. Monogamy in a person is not like the monogamy of geese or gibbons, in that it involves a vow of lifelong devotion, often conceived in sacramental terms.

The philosophical truth, that our kind is not a biological category, is swept out of view by the evolutionary and neuro-scientific picture of the human condition. It can be conjured back by stories, images and evocations, in something like the way that Milton conjured the truth of our condition from the raw materials of the Book of Genesis. Milton's allegory is not just a portrait of our kind; it is an invitation to kindness. It shows us what we are, and what we must live up to. And it sets a standard for art. Take away religion, however; take away philosophy, take away the higher aims of art, and you deprive ordinary people of the ways in which they can represent their apartness. Human nature, once something to live up to, becomes something to live down to instead. Biological reductionism nurtures this 'living down', which is why people so readily fall for it. It makes cynicism respectable and degeneracy chic. It abolishes our kind, and with it our kindness.

Among the most interesting of the concepts that inform and give structure to the human world is that of the face. The science of the human being has no real use for faces. Of course, it recognizes all the components of the face and their disposition in space. It acknowledges that there is such a thing as recognition of the face and facial agnosia. But it does not acknowledge the thing that makes faces so important to us – namely, that they are the outward form and image of the soul, the lamp lit in our world by the subject behind. It is through understanding the face that we begin to see how it is that subjects make themselves known in the world of objects.

4

The Face of the Person

The lamentation in Psalm 13 is expressed thus: 'How long wilt thou forget me, O Lord? For ever? How long wilt thou hide thy face from me?' In Psalm 17 we read 'As for me I will behold thy face in righteousness; I shall be satisfied, when I awake, with thy likeness'. The fourth psalm implores God to lift up 'the light of your countenance upon us'. Clearly we have moved a long way from the Torah. The hope of a face-to-face encounter fills the Psalms from beginning to end, and the hope is turned to a promise by the Apostle Paul, who tells us that now we see through a glass darkly, 'but then face to face'. God's face, which Moses was forbidden to see, is now at the centre of faith and hope, and the way to it, Paul says, is *agape*, the New Testament word for neighbour love, translated as *caritas* in the Vulgate and described by Kant as the 'love to which we are commanded'.

What is meant by the 'face of God'? This will be the theme of my remaining chapters. And the obvious starting point, given the argument of the last chapter, is the human face: what is it, exactly, what role does it play in inter-personal relations, and what is its fate in the age in which we live? The theme of the face is familiar from a certain kind of continental philosophy, and Emmanuel Levinas has devoted pages of tantalizing

73

obscurity to expounding it. The face, writes Levinas, is 'in and of itself visitation and transcendence':[1] and by this he seems to mean that the face comes *into* our shared world from a place beyond it, while in some way *remaining* beyond it, always just out of reach. This is the thought that I wish to explore. And I want to bring this all-important topic within the purview of philosophy as we know it in the English-speaking world – philosophy as argument, whose goal is truth. Levinas belongs to another tradition – the tradition of the prophets and mystics, who pursue dark thoughts at the edge of language, and who cast shadows over all that they approach.

Many animals have eyes, nostrils, lips and ears disposed in ways that resemble the disposition of the human face. And many animals recognize each other by their features. But would it be right to say that they have faces, and direct their attention to the face when relating to their companions? And what kind of questions are those? Can they be answered by empirical investigation, or are they bound up with ontological distinctions that lie deeper than the study of behaviour? In a famous book, Darwin set out to show that the expression of emotion in humans resembles its expression in other animals, and he gave examples that were supposed to show this.[2] The human face, he thought, is distinguished by its mobility, but not by its role in social communication. Emotions and motives are expressed in the face, so enabling other members of the species to anticipate behaviour, whether aggressive, appeasing, amorous, retreating or alarmed.

The dog, the swan and the person illustrated in Figure 1 display what Darwin took to be variations on a single pattern, in which teeth are bared or bill primed for attack, defences raised, and vulnerable features withdrawn for protection. Part

1. *Humanism of the Other*, trans. Nidra Poller, Chicago, University of Illinois Press, 2003, p. 44.
2. *The Expression of the Emotions in Man and Animals*, 1873.

of Darwin's purpose in showing such images was to indicate that our emotions are evolved responses, many of which we share with other species, and which reflect the background circumstances of our life as vulnerable organisms.

It is certainly true that faces, like any other part of the

Figure 1. Adapted from Darwin.

body, can display the forces that act on them – in that sense they can function as what the philosopher Paul Grice called 'natural signs'.[3] Grice expressly distinguished such natural signs from the human act of *meaning* something. Animals can read natural signs: a horse notices the laid back ears of its neighbour and gets out of the way; a dog recognizes the submissive gestures of its antagonist and ceases to fight. But this does not mean either that animals can *mean* things as we mean them, or that they see what we see, when we see the expression in a face. We have to ask ourselves what advantage it would be to an animal, that it could see faces, as well as the clues to future behaviour that they contain? Surely, none that we could fathom. The face, for us, is an instrument of meaning, and mediates between self and other in ways that are special to itself.

Grice's theory of meaning has spawned a vast literature that

3. H. P. Grice, 'Meaning', *The Philosophical Review,* 66, 1957, 377–88.

I must pass over here. But one central strand in his argument deserves mention. Grice was concerned to analyse the act of *meaning something* – 'speaker's meaning'. Meaning something involves an intentional action, but not all intentional actions are ways of meaning something. According to Grice, meaning involves an additional, 'second order', intention namely, the intention that the other should grasp the content of my action by recognizing that that is my intention. Leaving aside all subsequent refinements and qualifications, Grice's insight can be understood as capturing the I–You nature of meaning. In meaning something I am addressing you as another subject, with the intention that you recognize the subject in me. This immediately lifts what Grice called 'non-natural' meaning out of the repertoire of animal behaviour, and confers upon it a distinctively inter-subjective character.

The expression on a face is not normally intentional. An actor may intend his face to wear an expression of fear or anger: but the intention is to replicate what is unintentional. Nevertheless it is important that the face is the part of the body on which intention is inscribed, in the form of words, glances, nods and shakes. When we read the face we are aware of this. Facial expressions are where meaning lies; hence they serve as the natural sign of self-conscious and inter-personal states of mind.

Animals don't have the concept of the face – for this is a concept bound up with distinctions that only language users can make. But it does not follow that they don't recognize faces. After all no horse has the concept of a horse; but every horse recognizes horses, and is able to distinguish horse from non-horse in its environment. Animals are also able to discriminate objects on the basis of *Gestalten* – overall outline and similarity of form – even when this is not the result of a piecemeal similarity of parts. Birds are especially gifted in this respect and can recognize individual people on the basis of outline or facial features.[4] Nevertheless it seems redundant to describe an animal as recognizing something or someone by the face, rather than by the component features such as nose, brow, eyes and colouring. Maybe there are people who are like animals in this respect: who are unable to understand faces as *faces* but who yet recognize people by their features. Maybe such a person reasons (sub-consciously) as follows: long ears, wide-set eyes, large lips, high cheek-bones – yes, that's Bill. But such reasoning falls short of the capacity that we have, which is to see Bill *in* his face, and to see that face as a you and therefore an I. This capacity lies beyond the repertoire of birds and other animals. Nor, I would suggest, do the non-human apes possess it, even though they can 'recognize' themselves in mirrors – that is to say, understand from a mirror image that what they see there is some part of their own body.[5]

Hence you could imagine a person being face-blind as animals are face-blind, even if he is not blind to all the components that make up faces – perhaps some cases of prosopagnosia are like this. The case would resemble what Wittgenstein calls 'aspect blindness' – as when someone can see everything that composes the image in a picture but cannot see the image. (I suspect that 'tone deaf' people are like this: they hear all the sounds that compose the musical argument, but cannot hear the music that others hear *in* the sounds.) Seeing a face as a face means going beyond the physical features in some way, to a whole that emerges from

4. See *ScienceDaily*, May 19, 2009, for the case of mockingbirds. Corvids (crows, magpies, jackdaws etc.) are well known for their ability to recognize individuals belonging to other species than their own.
5. This was shown in a series of experiments by G. G. Gallup in 1970. See G. G. Gallup Jr, 'Chimpanzees: Self-recognition', *Science*, 167, 86–7. Since then several other species have been shown to pass the 'mirror test', notably dolphins. Researchers have often inferred from this that such animals therefore have the sense, and even the concept, of self. This inference is not licensed by the evidence, however.

them as a melody emerges from a sequence of pitched sounds, and which is, as Levinas aptly says, both a visitation and a transcendence.

I have an idea of transcendence from my own case. My face is one part of me that I do not see – unless, that is, I set *out* to see it, by using a mirror. People are surprised by their own face, in the way that they are not surprised by any other part of their body or by the face of another person. It is through the sight of their own face that they have the sense of what they are for others, and what they are *as* others. (They have this sense from hearing their own voice in a recording, and this too is the occasion of surprise and often discomfiture.) In the story of Narcissus the protagonist responds to himself as another, through confronting his own face. Until that moment he had been locked in himself – unable to acknowledge others and fleeing from their love. Tiresias had prophesied that Narcissus would live to a ripe old age if only 'he will not know himself'.[6] Catching sight of his own face in the pool Narcissus finds himself 'looked into' for the first time: he knows himself, but not *as* himself. He encounters a subject who flees from him as he had fled from others. And because he does not turn away, Narcissus is destroyed by what he sees.

My face is also the part of me to which others direct their attention, whenever they address me as 'you'. I lie *behind* my face, and yet I am present in it, speaking and looking through it at a world of others who are in turn both revealed and concealed like me. My face is a boundary, a threshold, the place where I appear as the monarch appears on the balcony of the palace. (Hence Dante's apt description, in the *Convivio*, of the eyes and the mouth as 'balconies of the soul'.) My face is therefore bound up with the pathos of my condition. In a sense you are always more clearly aware than I can be of what I am *in* the world; and when I confront my own face there

6. *Si se non noverit*, Ovid, *Metamorphoses*, III, 348.

may be a moment of fear, as I try to fit the person whom I know so well to this thing that others know better. How can the person, whom I know as a continuous unity from my earliest days until now, be identical with this decaying flesh that others have addressed through all its changes? This is the question that Rembrandt explored in his lifelong series of self-portraits. For Rembrandt the face is the place where the self and the flesh melt together, and where the individual is revealed not only in the life that shines on the surface but also in the death that is growing in the folds (Figure 2). The Rembrandt self-portrait is that rare thing – a portrait of the self. It shows the subject incarnate in the object, embraced by its own mortality, and present like death on the unknowable edge of things.

Figure 2. Rembrandt: Self Portrait.

When we speak of the person as lying *behind* his face we are speaking figuratively. Obviously he is not identical with his face; but that does not imply that he is wholly *other* than his face, still less that he is a clandestine soul, hidden behind the flesh like a clown behind his grease-paint. The natural signs that dogs read in the features of their fellow dogs are transparent effects of the passions that compel them. But the face of the human being is not in the same way transparent. People can deceive through their faces, and can use their faces to shape the world in their own favour. In *Macbeth* Duncan regrets having been taken in by the treacherous Thane of Cawdor, Macbeth's predecessor in that title, saying 'There is no art/ To find the mind's construction in the face': meaning that there is no way you can be instructed to discover what lurks behind a deceiving smile. The play proves Duncan right, since he is at once taken in by Macbeth, who murders him.

This possibility of deception arises precisely because we do not make a distinction, in our ordinary encounters, between a person and his face. When I confront another person face to face I am not confronting a physical part of him, as I am when, for example, I look at his shoulder or his knee. I am confronting *him*, the individual centre of consciousness, the free being who reveals himself in the face as another like me. There are deceiving faces, but not deceiving elbows or knees. When I read a face I am in some way acquainting myself with the way things seem to another person. And the expression on a face is already an offering in the world of mutual responsibilities: it is a projection in the space of inter-personal relations of a particular person's 'being there'. To put it in another way: the face is the subject, revealing itself in the world of objects.

That the face has this character is in part due to the larger significance of the human body. Thanks to our upright posture, our liberated forearms, and our all-seizing hands we are able to face things not merely with our eyes but with our whole being. This posture penetrates our intentional under-standing in subtle ways that have been in part clarified by Merleau-Ponty.[7] The human face announces the human body and precedes it like an ensign. And our reading of the face reflects this. The face occurs in the world of objects as though lit from behind. Hence it becomes the target and expression of our inter-personal attitudes, and looks, glances, smiles become the currency of our affections.

This means that the human face has a kind of inherent ambiguity. It can be seen in two ways – as the vehicle for the subjectivity that shines in it, and as a part of the human anatomy. The tension here comes to the fore in eating, as has been argued by Leon Kass and Raymond Tallis.[8] We do not, as animals do, thrust our mouths into our food in order to ingest it. We lift the food to our mouths, while retaining the upright posture that enables us to converse with our neighbours. In all societies (prior to the present) eating is a social occasion, with a pronounced ritual character, often preceded by a prayer of thanks. It occurs in a space that has been sanctified and ritualized, and into which the gods have been invited. All rituals impose discipline on the face, and this is part of what we experience when eating. However, the ordered nature of the food-to-face encounter goes beyond ritual discipline. Table manners have the function of maintaining the face and the mouth in their personal and conversational aspect. The well-mannered mouth is not just a mouth, and certainly not an aperture through which food is ingested. It is the place of the voice, the outlet of thought and feeling, a 'balcony of

7. *The Phenomenology of Perception*, 1945, trans. Colin Smith, London, Routledge and Kegan Paul, 1962. See also the excellent essay on our upright posture in Erwin Straus, *Phenomenological Psychology*, New York, Basic Books, 1966, and that by Raymond Tallis on the hand: *The Hand: A Philosophical Enquiry into Human Being*, Edinburgh, Edinburgh University Press, 2003.

8. Leon Kass, *The Hungry Soul: Eating and the Perfecting of Our Nature*, New York, Simon and Schuster, 1994; Raymond Tallis, *Hunger*, London, Acumen, 2008.

the soul'. And when people scoff greedily – especially when they do so in the solitary and needy manner that is becoming common – the mouth and the face change aspect, to become merely anatomical, their personal significance wiped out.

Of course, there is a balancing act here, and most people fall a little bit short, and indeed must fall short if they are not to appear prissy and precious at the dinner table. The crucial point is that even when serving a biological purpose, my face remains under my jurisdiction. It is the place where I am in the world of objects, and the place from which I address you. And the face has an interesting repertoire of adjustments, which cannot be understood merely as physical changes of the kind that we observe in the features of other species. For example there is smiling. Animals do not smile: at best they grimace, in the manner of chimpanzees and bonobos. In *Paradise Lost*, Milton writes (describing the love between Adam and Eve) that 'smiles from reason flow,/ To brute denied, and are of love the food'. The smile that reveals is the involuntary smile, the blessing that one soul confers upon another, when shining with the whole self in a moment of self-giving. Hence the voluntary and deliberately amplified smile is not a smile at all but a mask. One of the greatest smiles in all painting is that bestowed on Rembrandt by his aged mother, and by Rembrandt on her (see Figure 3). Here the mouth is barely inflected, and the eyes, dull with age, are nevertheless bright with maternal affection. Very few paintings present so vivid an instance, of the subject revealed in the face. We, the viewers, know what it is like for this woman, to look in this way on her son.

Smiling is one way of being present in the face; another way is kissing. Whereas a sincere smile is involuntary, a sincere kiss is willed. That is true, at least, of the kiss of affection. In the kiss of erotic passion, however, the will is also in part overcome and in this context the *purely* willed kiss has an air of *in*sincerity. The sincere erotic kiss is both an expression of will and a mutual surrender. Hence it requires a kind of

Figure 3. Rembrandt: The Artist's Mother.

government of the mouth, so that the soul can breathe out from it, and also surrender there, on the perimeter of one's being. Describing the temptation and fall of Francesca da Rimini, Dante writes of Francesca recalling the moment when she and Paolo read together the story of Lancelot and Guinevere, and reached the passage where Lancelot falls victim to Guinevere's smile. She remembers reading how the fond smile was 'kissed by such a lover'. She then recalls Paolo kissing, not her smile, for she was no longer smiling, but her mouth. And through her mouth she participates in Paolo's trembling: *la bocca mi baciò tutto tremante* (*Inferno*, V, 136). The mouth, like the eye, is a point of intersection of soul and body, person and animal. Francesca has been aware, through Guinevere, of her own smile, since she has been aware of the freedom of choice that is prompting her love. Then Paolo kisses her, and her smile becomes a mouth, full of trembling. She attributes this trembling to Paolo: and we sense how Francesca's self-image has been vanquished. She experiences her desire as a force from outside, an overcoming, which she is powerless to resist, since it has been transferred to the I.

The erotic kiss is not a matter of lips only: still more are the eyes and the hands involved. And surely Sartre is right to think that, in the caress of desire I am, as he puts it, seeking to 'incarnate the other' – in other words, I am seeking to bring into the flesh that I touch with my hands or lips, the thing that Sartre calls freedom, and which I am calling the first person perspective.[9] Sartre goes on to argue that sexual desire is inherently paradoxical, since it can succeed in its aim only by 'possessing another in his freedom' – in other words possessing another's freedom while also removing it. I don't agree with that. But I do think that the kiss of desire brings into prominence the very same ambiguity in the face that is present in eating. The lips offered by one lover to another are replete with subjectivity: they are the avatars of I, summoning the consciousness of another in a mutual gift. This is how the erotic kiss is portrayed by Canova, for example, in his sculpture of Eros and Psyche, Figure 4, and also by Rodin in 'The Kiss', a work that was originally called 'Paolo and Francesca'.

The lips are offered as spirit, but they respond as flesh. Pressed by the lips of the other they become sensory organs, bringing with them all the fatal entrapment of sexual pleasure, and ready to surrender to a force that breaks into the I from outside. Hence the kiss is the most important moment of desire – the moment in which soul and body are united, and in which lovers are fully face to face and also totally exposed

9. *L'Être et le néant: Essai d'ontologie phénoménologique*, Paris, Gallimard, 1943, Book III, Chapter 3. I discuss Sartre's views in *Sexual Desire*, London, Weidenfeld, and New York, Free Press, 1986, pp. 120–5.

Figure 4. Canova: Eros and Psyche.

to one another, in the manner that Francesca describes. The pleasure of the kiss is not a sensory pleasure: it is not a matter of sensations, but of the I–You intentionality and what it means. Hence there can be mistaken kisses, and mistaken pleasure in kissing, as was experienced by Lucretia, in Benjamin Britten and Ronald Duncan's version of the story, kissing the man she thought to be her husband, and whom she discovered to be the rapist Tarquin, though too late to defend herself.

The presence of the subject in the face is yet more evident in the eyes, and eyes play their part in both smiles and looks. Animals can look at things: they also look at each other. But they do not look *into* things. Perhaps the most concentrated of all acts of non-verbal communication between people is that of lovers, when they look into each other's eyes. They are not looking at the retina, or exploring the eye for its anatomical peculiarities, as an optician might. So what are they looking at or looking for? The answer is surely obvious: each is looking for, and hoping also to be looking at, the other, as a free subjectivity who is striving to meet him I to I.

To turn my eyes to you is a voluntary act. But what I then receive from you is not of my doing. As the symbol of all perception the eyes come to stand for that 'epistemic transparency' which enables the person to be revealed to another in his embodiment – as we are revealed in our looks, smiles, and blushes. The joining of perspective that is begun when a glance is answered with a blush or a smile finds final realization in wholly reciprocated glances: the 'me seeing you seeing me' of rapt attention, where neither of us can be said to be either doing or suffering what is done. Here is Donne's description:

> Our eye-beams twisted, and did thred
> Our eyes, upon one double string:
>   So to'entergraft our hands, as yet
> Was all the meanes to make us one,
>   And pictures in our eyes to get
> Was all our propagation.

Looks are voluntary. But the full revelation of the subject in the face is not, as a rule, voluntary. Milton's observation, that 'smiles from reason flow', is fully compatible with the fact that smiles are usually involuntary, and 'gift smiles', as one might call them, always so. Likewise laughter, to be genuine, must be involuntary – even though laughter is something of which only creatures with intentions, reason, and self-consciousness are capable. Laughter is a topic in itself, and I must pass over it here.[10] The important point is that, while

10. For pertinent discussion see Helmuth Plessner, *Laughing and Crying: A Study of the Limits of Human Behavior*, trans. James Spencer Churchill and Marjorie Grene, Evanston, Northwestern University Press, 1970, and F. H. Buckley, *The Morality of Laughter*, Ann Arbor, University of Michigan Press, 2003.

smiling and laughing are movements of the mouth, the whole face is infused by them, so that the subject is revealed in them as 'overcome'. The light grey eye of Isabel Archer, as Henry James describes her, 'had an enchanting softness when she smiled' – a softness that could be noticed only by the person who also saw the smile on her lips, and felt the change in her features as an involuntary outflow of pleasure.

Tears of merriment flow from the eyes, so too do tears of grief and pain. Hence tears are symbols of the spirit: it is as though something of me is lost with them. For this reason people have since ancient times felt the impulse to collect their tears in lachrymatories. Psalm 56, v. 8, laments to God 'Thou tellest my wanderings, put Thou my tears in Thy bottle; are they not in Thy Book?' Tears are like pains: they cannot be voluntary, even if you can do something else in order to produce them. Although there are actors and hypocrites who can produce tears at will, that does not make tears into intentional *actions*; it just means that there are ways of making the eyes water without producing 'real tears'. But laughing and smiling can be willed, and when they are willed they have a ghoulish, threatening quality, as when someone laughs cynically, or hides behind a knowing smile. Voluntary laughter may also be a kind of spiritual armour, with which a person defends himself against a treacherous world.

Similar observations apply to blushes, which are more like tears than laughter in that they cannot be intended. What Milton says about smiles could equally be said of blushes. Blushes from reason flow, to brute denied, and are of love the food. Only a rational being can blush, even though nobody can blush voluntarily. Even if, by some trick, you are able to make the blood flow into the surface of your cheeks, this would not be blushing but a kind of deception. And it is the involuntary character of the blush that conveys its meaning. Mary's blush upon meeting John, being involuntary, impresses him with the sense that *he* has summoned it – that it is in

some sense his doing, just as her smile is his doing. Her blush
is a fragment of her first person perspective, called up onto
the surface of her being and made visible in her face. In our
experience of such things our sense of the animal unity of the
other combines with our sense of his unity as a person, and
we perceive those two unities as an indissoluble whole. The
subject becomes, then, a real presence in the world of objects.

It is, I hope, not too fanciful to extend this phenomenology
of the face a little further, and to see the face as a symbol of
the individual and a display of his individuality. People are
individual animals; but they are also individual persons, and
as I argued in the last chapter, there is a puzzle as to how they
can be both. On one tradition – that associated with Locke –
the identity of the person through time is established by the
continuity of the 'I', and not by reference to the constancy of
the body. Although I don't accept this, I do accept that being a
person has something to do with the ability to remember the
past and intend the future, while holding oneself accountable
for both. And this connection between personality and the
first person case has in turn something to do with our sense
that human beings are individuals of a special kind and in
a special sense that distinguishes them from other spatio-
temporal particulars. The knowledge that I have of my own
individuality, which derives from my direct and criterionless
awareness of the unity that binds my mental states, gives
substance to the view that I am maintained in being as an
individual, through all conceivable change. The *Istigkeit* or
haecceitas is exemplified in me, as something that I cannot lose.
It is prior to all my states and properties and reducible to none
of them. In this I am god-like too. And it is this inner awareness
of absolute individuality that is translated into the face and
there made flesh. The eyes that look at me are your eyes, and
also you: the mouth that speaks and cheeks that blush are you.

The sense of the face as irradiated by the other and infused
with his self-identity underlies the power of masks in the

theatre. In the classical theatre of Greece, as in that of Japan, the mask was regarded not only as essential to the heightened tension of the drama, but also as the best way to guarantee that the emotions expressed by the words are reflected in the face. It is the spectator, gripped by the words, who sees their meaning shining in the mask. The impediment of human flesh and its imperfections has been removed, and the mask appears to change with every fluctuation of the character's emotions, to become the outward sign of inner feeling, precisely because the expression on the mask originates not so much in the one who wears it as in the one who beholds it. To make a mask that can be seen in this way requires skills acquired over a lifetime – perhaps more than a lifetime, the mask-makers of the Noh theatre of Japan handing on their art over many generations, and the best of the masks being retained in the private collections of patrons and performers, to be brought out only on occasions of the greatest solemnity.

The mask was a symbol of Dionysus, the god at whose festival the tragedies were performed. It did not signify the god's remoteness from the spectators – Dionysus was no *deus absconditus*. It signified his real presence among them. Dionysus was the god of tragedy and also the god of rebirth, conveyed by the wine into the soul of his worshippers, so as to include them in the dance of his own resurrection. The mask was the face of the god, sounding on the stage with the voice of human suffering, and sounding in the mystery cult with a divine and dithyrambic joy.

It is significant that the word 'person', which we borrow to express all those aspects of the human being associated with first-person awareness, came originally from the Roman theatre, where *persona* denoted the mask worn by the actor, and hence, by extension, the character portrayed.[11] By borrowing

---

11. There are conflicting etymologies: some say the word comes from Latin *per-sonare*, to sound through, others that the root is Etruscan, deriving from

the term the Roman law signified that, in a certain sense, we come always masked before judgement. As Sir Ernest Barker once put it: 'it is not the natural Ego which enters a court of law. It is a right-and-duty bearing person, created by the law, which appears before the law.'[12] The face, like the person, is both product and producer of judgement.

We should recognize too that it is not only in the theatre that masks are used. There are societies – that of Venice being the most singular – in which masks and masquerades have acquired complex functions that bring them into the very centre of communal life, to become indispensable items of clothing, without which people feel naked, indecent or out of place. In the Venetian Carnival the mask traditionally served two purposes: to cancel the everyday identity of the person, and also to create a new identity in its place – an identity *bestowed by the other*. Just as in the theatre the mask wears the expression projected onto it by the audience, so in the Carnival does the mask acquire its personality from the people all around. Hence, far from cutting people off from each other, the collective act of masking makes each person the product of others' interest: the moment of Carnival becomes the highest form of 'social effervescence', to use Durkheim's pregnant phrase.

In his remarkable study of the Venetian mask the historian James Johnson has explored the way in which, over many centuries, the role of the mask evolved, as one might put it, from *hiding* to *framing*. The Venetian mask became a way not of concealing the wearer but of endowing him with an 'incognito' presence; the mask was both transparent to his real identity and yet a barrier, a threshold, behind which he

the cult of Persephone, who was the principal subject of the Etruscan theatre, where she had a role resembling that of Dionysus in the Attic theatre.

12. Sir Ernest Barker, introduction to Otto Gierke, *Natural Law and the Theory of Society 1500–1800*, trans. Barker, Cambridge, Cambridge University Press, 1934, p. lxxi.

stood in a space of his own. At the height of its use, in the eighteenth-century Venice of Goldoni and Gozzi, the mask ceased to be a retreat from the world, and became instead a way of entering it, an instrument of freedom and a ceremonial acknowledgement of the public world. As Johnson puts it, the mask 'was a token of privacy instead of the real thing, a manufactured buffer that licensed genuine aloofness and unaccustomed closeness. Its ritualized "anonymity" could be acted on or ignored at will. The mask honoured liberty in the Venetian sense, which meant a measure of autonomy within jealously guarded limits'.[13]

The mask shows that the individualized face of the other is, in a certain measure, our own creation: remove the mask and beneath it you find a mask (Figure 5). This observation leads to a certain anxiety, since it suggests that the other's presence in his face may be no more real than his presence in the mask. Perhaps we are even mistaken in attributing to persons the kind of absolute individuality that we unavoidably see in their features. Maybe our everyday interactions are more 'carnivalesque' than we care to believe, the result of a constant and creative imagining that behind each face lies something like *this* – namely, the inner unity with which we are acquainted and for which none of us has words.[14] Maybe the individuality of the other resides *merely* in our way of seeing him, and has little or nothing to do with his way of *being*.

I am inclined to the view that there is no answer to the question what makes me the individual that I am that is not a trivial assertion of identity. But I am also inclined to the view that the notion of an absolute individuality arises spontaneously from the most fundamental inter-personal relations.

13. James H. Johnson, *Venice Incognito: Masks in the Serene Republic*, Berkeley, University of California Press, 2011, p. 128.
14. We owe the word 'carnivalesque', used to describe a comprehensive attitude to reality, to Mikhail Bakhtin, *Rabelais and His World*, trans. Hélène Iswolsky, Bloomington, Indiana University Press, 1993.

Figure 5. Lorenzo Lippi: Woman with Mask and Pomegranate.

It is implied in all our attempts at integrity and responsible living. And it is built into our way of perceiving as well as our way of describing the human world. Rather than dismiss it as an illusion, I would prefer to say that it is a 'well-founded phenomenon', in Leibniz's sense, a way of seeing the world that is indispensable to us, and which we could never have conclusive reason to reject.

Moreover, the face has this meaning for us because it is the threshold at which the other appears, offering 'this thing that I am' as a partner in dialogue. This feature goes to the heart of what it is to be human. Our inter-personal relations would be inconceivable without the assumption that we can commit ourselves through promises, take responsibility now for some event in the future or the past, make vows that bind us forever to the one who receives them, and undertake obligations that we regard as untransferable to anyone else. And all this we read in the face.

Especially do we read those things in the face of the beloved in the look of love. Our sexual emotions are founded on individualizing thoughts: it is *you* whom I want and not the type or pattern. This individualizing intentionality does not merely stem from the fact that it is persons (in other words, individuals) whom we desire. It stems from the fact that the other is desired as an embodied subject, and not as a body.[15] And the embodied subject is what we see in the face.

You can see the point by drawing a contrast between desire and hunger. Suppose that people were the only edible things; and suppose that they felt no pain on being eaten and were reconstituted at once. How many formalities and apologies would now be required in the satisfaction of hunger! People would try to conceal their appetite, and learn not to presume upon the consent of those whom they surveyed with famished glances. It would become a crime to partake of a meal without the meal's consent. Maybe marriage would be the best solution. Still, this predicament is nothing like the predicament in which we are placed by desire. It arises from

15. I have defended this point at length in *Sexual Desire: A Moral Philosophy of the Erotic, op. cit.* The notion of the 'embodied subject' is also fundamental to the analysis of perception given by Merleau-Ponty.

the lack of anything impersonal to eat, but not from the nature of hunger. Hunger is directed towards the other only as object, and any similar object will serve just as well. It does not individualize the object, or propose any other union than that required by need. Still less does it require of the object those intellectual, moral and spiritual virtues that the lover might reasonably demand – and, according to the literature of courtly love, must demand – in the object of his desire.

When sexual attentions take the form of hunger they become deeply insulting. And in every form they compromise not only the person who addresses them, but also the person addressed. Precisely because desire proposes a relation between subjects, it forces both parties to account for themselves: it is an expression of my freedom, which seeks out the freedom in you. Hence modesty and shame are part of the phenomenon – a recognition that the 'I' is on display in the body, and its freedom in jeopardy. This we see clearly in Rembrandt's painting of Susanna and the Elders, Figure 6, in which Susanna's body is made to shrink into itself by the prurient eyes that observe her, like the flesh of a mollusc from which the shell has been prised.

Unwanted advances are therefore also forbidden by the one to whom they might be addressed, and any transgression is felt as a contamination. That is why rape is so serious a crime: it is an invasion of the victim's freedom, and a dragging of the subject into the world of things. I don't need to emphasize the extent to which our understanding of desire has been influenced and indeed subverted by the literature, from Havelock Ellis through Freud to the Kinsey reports, which has purported to lift the veil from our collective secrets. But it is worth pointing out that if you describe desire in the terms that have become fashionable – as the pursuit of pleasurable sensations in the private parts – then the outrage and pollution of rape become impossible to explain. Rape, on this view, is every bit as bad as being spat upon: but no worse. In fact, just about

Figure 6. Rembrandt: Susanna and the Elders.

everything in human sexual behaviour becomes impossible to explain – and it is only what I have called the 'charm of disenchantment' that leads people to receive the now fashionable descriptions as the truth.

Rape is not just a matter of unwanted contact. It is an existential assault and an annihilation of the subject. This fact has seldom been more poignantly captured than by Goya, in one of his paintings devoted to scenes of brigandage. The girl in this painting (Figure 7) is being relieved of her clothes by her captors, who handle the precious stuff with a concupiscent delicacy that is all the more excruciating in that we know how they are about to handle her. She hides from them, not her body but her face, the place where her shame is revealed, and by hiding which she does all that she can to withdraw herself from what is about to happen.

Sexual desire is inherently compromising, and the choice to express it or to yield to it is an existential choice, in which the self is at risk. Not surprisingly, therefore, the sexual act is surrounded by prohibitions; it brings with it a weight of shame, guilt and jealousy, as well as joy and happiness. Sex is therefore deeply implicated in the sense of original sin, as I described it earlier: the sense of being sundered from what we truly are, by our fall into the world of objects.

There is an important insight contained in the book of Genesis, concerning the loss of *eros* when the body takes over. Adam and Eve have partaken of the forbidden fruit, and obtained the 'knowledge of good and evil' – in other words the ability to invent for themselves the code that governs their behaviour. God walks in the garden and they hide, conscious for the first time of their bodies as objects of shame. This 'shame of the body' is an extraordinary feeling, and one that no animal could conceivably have. It is a recognition of the body as in some way alien – the thing that has wandered into the world of objects as though of its own accord, to become the victim of uninvited glances. Adam and Eve have become conscious that they are not only face to face, but joined in another way, as bodies, and the objectifying gaze of lust now poisons their once innocent desire. Milton's description of this transition, from the pure *eros* that preceded the fall, to the polluted lust that followed it, is one of the great psychological triumphs in English literature. But how brilliantly

Figure 7. Goya: Scene of Brigandage.

and succinctly does the author of Genesis cover the same transition! By means of the fig leaf Adam and Eve are able to rescue each other from the worst: to ensure, however tentatively, that they can still be face to face, even if the erotic has now been privatized and attached to the private parts.

In his well-known fresco of the expulsion from Paradise, Masaccio shows the distinction between the two shames – that of the body, which causes Eve to hide her sexual parts, and that of the soul, which causes Adam to hide his face (Figure 8). Like the girl in Goya's picture, Adam hides the *self*; Eve shows the self in all its confused grief, but still protects the body – for that, she now knows, can be tainted by others' eyes.

I have dwelt on the phenomenon of the erotic because it illustrates the importance of the face, and what is conveyed by the face, in our personal encounters, even in those encounters motivated by what many think to be a desire that we share with other animals, and which arises directly from the reproductive strategies of our genes. In my view sexual desire, as we humans experience it, is an inter-personal response – one that presupposes self-consciousness in both subject and object, and which singles out its target as a free and responsible individual, able to give and withhold at will. It has its perverted forms, but it is precisely the inter-personal norm that enables us to describe them as perverted. Sexual relations between members of other species have, materially speaking, much in common with those between people. But from the intentional point of view they are entirely different. Even those creatures who mate for life, like wolves and geese, are not animated by promises, by devotion that shines in the face, or by the desire to unite with the other, who is another like me. Human sexual endeavour is morally weighted, as no animal endeavour can be. And its focus on the individual is mediated by the thought of that individual as a *subject*, who freely chooses, and in whose first person pespective I appear

Figure 8. Masaccio: Expulsion from Paradise.

as he or she appears in mine. To put it simply, and in the language of the Torah, human sexuality belongs in the realm of the covenant.

Someone might respond by saying that I have described what is at best an ideal, and that the reality may be very different. Our world abounds in sexual practices that ignore or by-pass the subjectivity of the other – sexual encounters in dark rooms where the face cannot be seen, encounters with 'real dolls' that respond with a caricature of human excitement, encounters imagined through the screen or vicariously enjoyed through pornography, voyeurism and video sex-games. But I would reply that, in almost all cases where we do not refer directly to perversion (as in bestiality and necrophilia) the object of sexual interest is being treated as a *substitute*: the object is the imaginary other, the fantasy subject, and serves a sexual purpose precisely by being tied in my imagination to the real desiring me. Objects can be *substitutes* for subjects as the target of sexual excitement, but they cannot replace them. It is not the shoe that the fetishist desires, but the imaginary woman with whose aura it is filled.

Hence there is an important sense in which human sexual desire is non-transferable: to the person wanting Jane it is absurd to say 'take Elizabeth, she will do just as well'; for what he wants to do is an action in which Jane is a constituent, and not just an instrument. True, Elizabeth could be *substituted* for Jane, as Leah was substituted for Rachel in the Old Testament story of Jacob's marriage (Gen. 29.21-28). But Jacob's desire was not transferred to Leah: he simply made a mistake, believing her to be Rachel. It is true too that you can desire more than one person, or move promiscuously from one person to the next. But there is a deep difference between orgiastic sex, in which the other is relevant only as a means, and serial seduction, in which the inter-personal intentionality of desire is maintained in truncated form. Consider Don Juan. The essence of his personality is seduction, and seducing means eliciting consent, through representing your own consuming interest in doing so. Don Juan is seductive because he feels passion for every woman he meets, and yet his passion is not transferable. It would be absurd to break into his seduction of Zerlina (in the version that we owe to Da Ponte and Mozart) with the announcement 'take this one, she will do just as well' (hence the pathos of Donna Elvira's interruption). This point is made clear by Casanova in his *Memoirs*, in which his intense and interrogatory desire singles out each object in turn for the very person that she is, and for whom no other could possibly be a substitute – which is why Casanova was irresistible. If we thought of desire merely as a kind of hunger, satisfied now by this human burger, now by that, it would make sense to think of it as transferable. But, as I have suggested, even in the pathological cases like those of Don Juan and Casanova, it is the interest in the other that is the intentional heart of desire – and in the other as an embodied person, with a unique subjectivity that defines his or her point of view.

In a once widely read book, *Eros and Agape*, the Swedish Protestant theologian Anders Nygren made a radical distinction between erotic love, which is motivated by its object, and the Christian love commended by St Paul in the first letter to the Corinthians, ch. 13, which is motivated by God. Greek distinguishes the two as *eros* and *agape*, we as romantic love and neighbour-love. And a great change came over the world, in Nygren's view, when *agape* replaced *eros*, as the raw material for the love of God. In Plato *eros* arises in a god-like way – that is to say, as an external and invading force, which overwhelms the psyche. But it ascends like a fire, and carries the subject heavenward, to the realm of the forms which is the kingdom of God. St Paul, by contrast, emphasizes *agape*, which comes to us *from* God, rather than raising us *to* him. The downward turning love of the almighty fills us with gratitude, and we reciprocate by spreading it outwards to our neighbours here on earth.

It would certainly be a mistake to confound *eros* and *agape*. Sexual love is not in itself a benefit conferred on the target: it may well be an affliction. Sexual love desires to possess, and usually to possess exclusively – or at least with an alert distrust of rivals. Sexual love can be cruel and full of anger; it has an ambivalent relation to moral virtue, and in certain forms – such as that described by Jean Genet in *Le Journal du voleur* and *Nôtre Dame des fleurs* – is inspired and excited by vice. It makes massive and unfair discriminations between the beautiful and the ugly, the strong and the weak, the young and the old. It is jealous, and cannot rejoice in the good things given by a rival. A person can murder the object of erotic love as Othello did, and when people fall in love they are aware that they are embarking on a path that is as much a threat to the social order as a natural fruit of it. Hence lovers are furtive; they conceal their feelings, knowing that the world is as likely to be angered as pleased by the sight of their attachment.[16]

None of those things is true of *agape* (charity), and no society could be founded on erotic love as a society might be founded on the love of neighbour. Hence *eros* is a danger: it is a force that undermines trust as much as it builds trust, and the greatest danger is that it might become detached entirely from inter-personal relations and returned to its animal origins. This is what Plato feared, and why he developed his theory of what we now know as Platonic love – maybe the most influential psychological theory in history. For Plato the physical urge must be overcome, so that the desire directed to the beautiful boy can be redirected to its proper object, which is the form of the beautiful itself.

Plato's mistake was to think that normal sexual desire is directed towards the beautiful body, rather than towards the embodied subject. The solution to the problem of desire is not to overcome it, but to ensure that it retains its personal focus. A society based on *agape* alone is all very well, but it will not reproduce itself: nor will it produce the crucial relation – that between parent and child – which is the basis on which we can begin to understand our relation to God. Hence the redemption of the erotic lies at the heart of every viable social order – a fact well understood by traditional religions, all of which see sexual union as a 'rite of passage' in which society as a whole is involved, and which brings about an existential change in those whom it joins. This existential change requires a blessing, so as to be lifted from the realm of mutual appetite and remade as a spiritual union.

On the Cathedral of Reims there is affixed the sculpture

---

16. Schopenhauer makes much of this point in the essay on sexual love, in *The World as Will and Representation*, vol. 2.

Figure 9. Reims Cathedral: Smiling Angel.

of an angel, Figure 9, whose smile is intended to represent the love of God for men – the downward-tending, all comprehending love of *agape*. The sculptor has tried to represent the kind of existential support that we receive, on the Christian view, from God. He wishes to display the essence of love as Aquinas described it – the willing of another's good.[17] In the Thomist view love and friendship are to be understood as *endorsements* – ways of saying to another that 'your being is my desire'. For this very reason, however, the smile on the angel's face makes us uncomfortable. It is not the tender smile, the smile of the flesh, that one lover confers on another or that a mother confers on her child. It has a willed and abstract quality. This smile has

17. *Summa Theologiae*, 2a 2ae, qqs 25–8.

not been 'called forth' onto the angel's face by the particular person who is its object, for *agape* makes no distinctions, and may have no particular person in mind. Hence the smile has a double aspect: now it seems deliberate and therefore false, now involuntary and therefore replete with unearthly benevolence.

There is a truth in Aquinas's view of love, that it involves willing the other's good. But only *some* kinds of love are like that. Erotic love may desire the non-being of its object just as much as the being – something that we surely did not need Wagner's *Tristan und Isolde* to show us. If I feel erotic love for another, I endorse her being for my sake as much as for hers. And the circumstances might arise in which my endorsement is withdrawn: like Othello, I might, in a passion of jealousy, seek her destruction. If I feel neighbour love for her, then my endorsement is entirely for *her* sake. It is unconditional in a way that erotic love can never be. Yet more unconditional, of course, is the love than shines in the old face of Rembrandt's mother, who quietly and unassumingly makes a gift of herself to her son. The angel is not making a gift of himself: he is relaying the love of God. And although Christians believe that God also made a gift of himself, through Christ, this is a peculiarity of the Christian religion that is not reflected in the account of God's love that we are given in the other Abrahamic faiths.

On one Christian understanding marriage is a sacrament – which means a union forged in the presence of God. And the purpose of the sacrament is to incorporate *eros* into the world of *agape* – to ensure that the face of the lover can still be turned to the world of others. Human societies differ in the way that they manage this, and some don't even attempt it. But the purpose, where it exists, is everywhere the same: to ensure that the private face of the lover can at a moment become the public face of the citizen, or the outgoing face of the friend. Hence where marriage is not regarded as a sacrament, but merely as a contract between the husband and the parents of the bride, the face of the wife often remains hidden after marriage: marriage does nothing to lift her from the private to the public forms of love. That is the *deep* explanation of the *burqa*: it is a way of underlining the exclusion of women from the public sphere. They can appear there as a bundle of clothing, but never as a face: to be fully a person the woman must retreat into the private sphere, where *eros*, rather than *agape*, is sovereign.

The Thomistic idea of love, as willing the being and the flourishing of another, assumes a kind of existential separation between the lover and the beloved. I will your being by willing you to be *other* than me. In erotic love, however, there is an existential tie: the partners are *bound up* in each other (as we say 'involved'), and this is an impediment to the attitude described by St Thomas. I do not will my lover to be wholly *other* than me, and I am not 'happy for him', as I am happy for others when they obtain something that they desire. And this is a partial explanation of the fact noted earlier, that lovers do not look at each other, but look *into* each other, and search the eyes and face of the beloved for the thing to which they seek to be united (and with which they can never really be united, since it is not a thing but a perspective, defined for all eternity as *other* than mine). C. S. Lewis puts the point nicely with his remark that friends are side by side, while lovers are face to face.[18]

Perhaps that goes some way towards explaining why it is that the great mystics and religious poets, when they endeavour to describe the love that the soul has for God, almost always follow Plato's example, and take erotic love as their analogical base. This is true of St John of the Cross, of St Teresa of Avila, of Rumi and Hafiz. For the love of God is also an acknowledgement of total existential dependence,

18. *The Four Loves*, London, Harvest Books, 1960.

of the nothingness of my being until completed by him. Maybe his love coming down to me and through me to my fellow men is *agape*. But mine that aspires to him, and seeks him out in utter servitude, is more like *eros*, a condition of existential need. In the extreme forms of ecstasy, whether religious or sexual, the face is in fact eclipsed, the self utterly expelled from it, wandering as it were outside the body, and this is what we see in the face of St Teresa as Bernini depicted her, Figure 10. This is a face no longer inhabited by the self, like a place abandoned and falling into ruin.

In conclusion, it is appropriate to say something about the destiny of the face, in the world that we have entered – a world in which *eros* is being rapidly detached from inter-personal commitments and redesigned as a commodity. The first victim of this process is the face, which has to be subdued to the

Figure 10. Bernini: St Teresa in Ecstasy.

rule of the body, to be shown as overcome, wiped out or spat upon. The underlying tendency of erotic images in our time is to present the body as the focus and meaning of desire, the place where it all occurs, in the momentary spasm of sensual pleasure of which the soul is at best a spectator, and no part of the game. In pornography the face has no role to play, other than to be subjected to the empire of the body. Kisses are of no significance, and eyes look nowhere since they are searching for nothing beyond the present pleasure. All this amounts to a marginalization, indeed a kind of desecration, of the human face. And this desecration of the face is also a cancelling out of the subject. Sex, in the pornographic culture, is not a relation between subjects but a relation between objects. And anything that might enter to impede that conception of the sexual act – the face in particular – must be veiled, marred or spat upon, as an unwelcome intrusion of judgement into a sphere where everything goes. All this is anticipated in the pornographic novel, *Histoire d'O*, in which enslaved and imprisoned women are instructed to ignore the identity of the men who enjoy them, to submit their faces to the penis, and to be defaced by it.[19]

A parallel development can be witnessed in the world of sex idols. Fashion models and pop stars tend to display faces that are withdrawn, scowling and closed. Little or nothing is given through their faces, which offer no invitation to love or companionship. The function of the fashion-model's face is to put the body on display; the face is simply one of the body's attractions, with no special role to play as a focus of another's interest. It is characterized by an almost metaphysical vacancy, as though there is no soul inside, but only, as Henry James once wrote, a dead kitten and a ball of string. How we have arrived at this point is a deep question that I must here pass over. But one thing is certain, which is that things were not

19. Anon. (Anne Desclos) *Histoire d'O*, Paris, Pauvert, 1954.

always so. Sex symbols and sex idols have always existed. But seldom before have they been faceless.

One of the most famous of those symbols, Simonetta Vespucci, mistress of Lorenzo da Medici, so captured the heart of Botticelli that he used her as the model for his great painting of the Birth of Venus (Figure 11). In the central figure the body has no meaning other than the diffusion and outgrowth of the soul that dreams in the face – anatomically it is wholly deformed, and a girl who actually looked like this would have no chance in a modern fashion parade. Botticelli is presenting us with the true, Platonic *eros*, as he saw it – the face that shines with a light that is not of this world, and which invites us to transcend our appetites and to aspire to that higher realm where we are united to the forms – Plato's version of a world in which the only individuals are souls. Hence the body of Botticelli's Venus is subservient to the face,

Figure 11. Botticelli: Birth of Venus (detail).

a kind of caricature of the female anatomy which nevertheless takes its meaning from the holy invitation that we read in the eyes above.

Botticelli's Venus is not a sex-object, but a sex-subject. The intrusion of the sex-object into art can be already witnessed in the salon art of nineteenth-century France. Witness Bouguereau's brilliantly accomplished, Ingres-inspired and entirely saccharine Birth of Venus, in which vapid sensual faces stare vacantly at the goddess, as she turns her face from the spectator in order to sniff her freshly shaven armpit and to toy narcisistically with her hair (Figure 12). It would be unfair to dismiss this painting as pornographic. But there is no subject, only a void, within this Venus of flesh.

Botticelli's great picture reminds us that the human face is to be understood in quite another way from the body-parts of an animal. Animals do not see faces, since they cannot see that which *organizes* eyes, nose, mouth and brow as a face – namely the self, whose residence those features are. It is in part from our experience of the face that we understand our world as illuminated by freedom. The face is therefore not just an object among objects, and when people invite us to perceive it as such, in the manner of the fashion model and the pop star, they succeed only in defacing the human form. This defacing is something that we witness all around us, and it is also experienced – especially in its sexual application – as a desecration. In my view it is no accident that we are disposed to speak of desecration when it comes to sex. We can desecrate only what is sacred. And in describing the role of the face in inter-personal relations I have been taking the first steps towards a theory of the sacred.

Levinas writes of the face as the absolute obstacle to murder, the sight of which causes the assassin's hand to drop. Would that Levinas's remark were true. But there is *a* truth contained in it. Through the face the subject appears in our world, and it appears there haloed by prohibitions. It is untouchable,

Figure 12. Bouguereau: Birth of Venus.

inviolable, consecrated. It is not to be treated as an object, or
to be thrown into the great computer and calculated away.
Levinas wrote in torment, thinking of the murder of his own
friends and family in the holocaust. And it is surely an apt
description of the genocides of the twentieth century that they
proceeded as they did only because subjects were first reduced
to objects, so that all faces disappeared. That was the work
of the concentration camp, and it is a work that has been

described for all time by Primo Levi, Solzhenitsyn and the angelic Nijole Sadunaite – people who kept their faces, even in face of the all-defacing machine.

Nobody could say that the growth of the pornographic culture is a crime comparable to the crimes described by those writers, though, like those crimes, it is a crime against humanity.[20] Nevertheless pornography has moved of its own accord to that first stage on the road to desecration – the stage of objectification, in which the face disappears, and the human being disintegrates into an assemblage of body parts. My own view is that we should see this as a warning. What to do about it, and what it means for us, are questions to which I return. But my remarks will only make proper sense, I think, if I move on to consider another kind of face against which the spirit of desecration is currently active: the face of the earth, as we humans have built it.

20. How would I justify that charge? See Donna M. Hughes and James R. Stoner (eds), *The Social Costs of Pornography: A Collection of Papers*, Princeton, Witherspoon Institute, 2010.

5

The Face of the Earth

In his encounter with Moses God makes three things clear to his people. First, he is a person. Secondly, there is a body of rules and covenants, by which we can live in peace with him. Thirdly, we must make room for him among us, by building a temple as his home. In this chapter I want to turn my attention to the third of those declarations.

In studying the human face I was exploring some part of what it means to say that persons reveal themselves in the world. The real presence of the person, I argued, brings the search for righteousness and the possibility of guilt, since it means that we live under the eyes of strangers, and are judged by them. And when we seek refuge in intimacy, so as to look into eyes that look into ours, we are confronted with a peculiar moral barrier. *Eros* is not a place of ordinary safety, but a sanctuary, a precinct threatened by pollution and protected by taboo. The temptation is to enter this place in a spirit of iconoclasm, destroying or masking the face. That, I suggested, is the familiar path of desecration, which brings neither peace nor love. For love is a relation between subjects, and when people become objects for each other, love withers and dies. The result of this defacing of the erotic is not hatred, but an ever-expanding heartlessness.

The destiny of *eros* in our time reminds us of the many other ways in which we seek the guiltless place, the place free from adverse judgement. In the Torah God's gift of laws and covenants shows the path to that place – it guides us in the way of the Lord. But law in the Hebrew Bible does not stand alone, nor are God's commandments offered as though arbitrary, and without foundation in the personal relations that God upholds and claims. On the contrary, the law is connected from the outset with the concept of neighbour love, the love that St Paul calls *agape* and which (to use Kant's idiom) is commanded as a law.

Hence the law of the Torah is not an unexplained path. It is not like the Koran, a record of God's arbitrary will, for which he is not accountable. The law of the Torah is entirely bound up with God's identity as a person, and in the Psalms and the book of Job God is called to account by his faithful servants and asked to explain himself. Jacob acquired the name 'Israel' (one who 'wrestles with God') through his encounter with the angel of the Lord (Gen. 32; Hos. 12). And the people that took Jacob's name continue to wrestle with the God who chose them. Through the law God is putting relations with his creatures on an inter-personal footing, and making clear that his law, in the end, establishes the righteous life – the life free from guilt, in which we are at one with each other and with our own being-in-the-world.

Moreover, because God responds to my cry, I can regain his path when I have strayed from it. 'Create in me a clean heart, O God; and renew a right spirit within me,' implores the Psalmist (Ps. 51), adding that 'the sacrifices of God are a broken spirit; a broken and a contrite heart, O God, thou wilt not despise'. Repentance is bound into our relation with the God of Moses: as in a marriage, it is by asking forgiveness that we recapture the averted face.

All that must be borne in mind as we turn to God's third declaration: that he requires a home in this world, a temple in which the architecture and the rituals convey a clear conception of his nature and his presence.

It is a notable feature of the Old Testament narrative that it makes frequent reference to sacred places. The patriarchs erect altars, make sacrifices, bestow names on places rendered holy by some encounter with God and his angels. Nor should this surprise us. The idea of the sacred place seems to be a human universal. Different accounts are given to explain it. For some cultures gods, spirits and other supernatural agents live among us, and must be worshipped or acknowledged at the spot where they reside. For others a place becomes sacred because it is the haunt of a ghost, maybe the ghost of someone who has died with some deep need unsatisfied or some deep love denied, and whose moment of crisis occurred at this very spot: this idea you find in the Shinto religion, and dramatized in the Noh theatre of Japan. Our sorrows, Rilke wrote, are '*nicht nur/ Zeit – sind Stelle, Siedelung, Lager, Boden, Wohnort*' (tenth Duino Elegy): they are not time only – they are place, settlement, camp, ground, dwelling. Sorrows *inhabit* the world, and haunt the places where they once were suffered.

Other cultures connect sacred places with the legends of heroes or with great battles of the past, to which we come to pay respects for some patriotic sacrifice. In all societies in which dead people are ceremonially buried, the place of burial becomes 'hallowed ground', and ritualized acts and words are deemed appropriate when we walk there. Funerary rites, beliefs about the gods and the afterlife, invocations of ancestors and declarations of solidarity with the dead and the unborn – these are the core experiences from which lasting cultures derive, and they find expression in graveyards and tombs at every age and in every place. In a thoughtful book Ken Worpole has recorded the astonishing variety of attempts to render death acceptable after the event, through the architecture, landscaping and rituals of the cemetery. And, as he shows, it is in cemeteries that people have shown most cogently their respect for the landscape and the earth.[1] It is here, even in an age of religious decline and public scepticism, that the sense of the sacred still lingers and extends its protecting hand.

A comparable sentiment attaches to ruins, and it is from the attempt to represent ruins and their meaning that our tradition of landscape painting began. The imaginary ruins of Piranesi and Canaletto, the reconstructed ruins of Poussin and Claude, the picturesque castles of Richard Wilson – all show the landscape as haunted by people for whom it was once, in some great trauma or emergency, *here* and *now*. Painters may anticipate ruins, in the manner of Hubert Robert, rescuing a building from the present by showing its future state of decay. Our monuments, Robert reminds us, are both ways to remember and signs that we forget. Ruins are the enigmatic fragments of a life that can never again be reassembled. And because they blend into the landscape they endow the natural world with the face of the many dead.

The sacred place is a place that has been singled out by suffering or sacrifice, by revelation or prayer. It is marked by a stone, an altar or a shrine, and is a place of pilgrimage. Pilgrimage may be a sacred duty, like the *hajj*, a search for healing, like the trek to St James of Compostella, or a penitence, like the journey to Canterbury, ending on hands and knees, that purged the crime of Henry II. It may belong to a specific religion, to many religions, like 'the Golden Road to Samarkand', or to none. Richard Jefferies, who walked the earth in search of the intense self-communing that he described as 'prayer', referred to his walks as 'pilgrimages' (*The Story of My Heart*), and found in their fleeting destinations a revelation of his own soul, blended with the soul-stuff of the universe.

1. Ken Worpole, *Last Landscapes: The Architecture of Cemeteries in the West*, London, Reaktion Books, 2003.

In this chapter I want to explore the emotions and motives that lead us to respect some place as holy or in some related way protected from violation, and which govern our sense that there are right and wrong ways to treat the earth on which we live and build. It is clear that this theme was fundamental to the Israel of the Patriarchs. Their world was very different from ours, far less densely populated, far more dangerous (at least in matters of day-to-day life) and far less subject to abuse. But they, like us, were conscious of the uniqueness of their territory, of the need to respect it and to sanctify it. They regarded the Promised Land not as a thing to consume and discard but as an inheritance, to be cared for and passed on. And this feeling was bound up for them with two others: their conviction that God was a real presence among them, and their sense of the land as a gift – not a gift to the present generation to use as it will, but a gift to a people in its entirety and for all time, a resource to be renewed and passed on. And this records a general truth about the sacred. Sacred places are protected from spoliation; they are steeped in the hopes and the sufferings of those who have fought for them. And they belong to others who are yet to be. This, to my way of thinking, is a paradigm of environmental protection, and one that we must again understand, if we are to come to grips with what is happening, as our world is defaced by the habit of consuming it.

Readers of Pausanias, the second-century geographer and traveller, will notice that the temples of the gods, the sacred groves and the tombs of heroes were still intact when Pausanias visited them, maintained as public assets by priests and devotees of the old religion, in those last years before Christianity swept everything away. Piety forbad their destruction, and it is piety that animated Pausanias in visiting them and recording their charms. This motive is a human universal, and as Simon Schama has argued, in his eloquent tribute to landscape art and to the myths and mysteries of settlement, land and landscape have been portrayed as sacred in all our human attempts to belong in the world.[2]

This experience of sanctity is deeply tied to memory. We carry within us the after-image of primeval attachments. Memory corrects and straightens our recollections, and shapes the remembered *oikos* in terms that are as much imagined as real. We see the process whereby a lost home becomes sacred, and purged of all its irritating ordinariness, in Mickiewicz's invocation of old Lithuania (*Pan Tadeusz*), and Proust's invocation of Combray. And we recognize in those literary *tours de force* a tribute to another relation with the world than the one into which we have been trapped by the habits of consumption. The world described by Proust looks back at him from his own eyes. It is not just a world of objects to be used and discarded. It is a world of *revealed meanings*, in which the most ordinary thing might suddenly blurt out its secrets, or in which a landscape can burst into tears.

Such a sentiment tied the Israelites to the Promised Land, and to the Holy City that was built in it. Hence, in addition to the ten commandments, God presented Moses with the design for a sanctuary, 'that I may dwell among them' (Exod. 25.8). The elaborate instructions fix the architecture and the ritual of the Temple, and it is around this temple that the city of Jerusalem was built – the shining city on the hill that is the sacred place to which God's people turn from their tribulations. By the time of the Psalms the sanctity of the temple and that of the city have become one – for the true settlement is one in which God dwells among us, and its destruction is an act of sacrilege that changes the face of the world. Surely no one can doubt that the emotion that attaches human subjects to their sacred places is their deepest intimation of what it means to be *in* the world, and in dialogue with it:

2. Simon Schama, *Landscape and Memory*, New York, Alfred Knopf, 1995.

If I forget thee, O Jerusalem,
Let my right hand forget her cunning.
If I do not remember thee
Let my tongue cleave to the roof of my mouth;
If I prefer not Jerusalem above my chief joy.

The spoiling of the earth and the vandalizing of our human habitats arouse in us an echo of the desolation that the psalmist records: the desolation that ensues, when the spiritual resource on which we depend is driven from its sanctuary, and the sanctuary destroyed. And it seems to me that we will not understand what is really at stake in the environmental consciousness that has captured the imagination of so many people today, if we do not recognize a religious memory at the heart of it. God's message concerning the temple was not simply the foundation of a specific cult, devoted to the god of a tribe. It was a message to all of us, telling us that God will dwell among us only if we too dwell, and that dwelling does not mean consuming the earth or wasting it, but conserving it, so as to make a lasting sanctuary for both God and man. Hence the promise of God's kingdom in the book of Revelation is a promise of the 'New Jerusalem', the Holy City, in which we live side by side and face to face with God. And the theme of the Holy City, which is the measure and ideal of all our settlements, was made central to Christian life by St Augustine, in *The City of God*. We might summarize the message concerning the temple thus: a true city begins from an act of consecration, and it is the temple, God's dwelling, which is the model for all other dwellings. It is from the temple that we can learn how to build.

The temple is doubly sacred. Not only is it consecrated to God; it also contains him. It is the place where he is, and where the faithful can encounter him. But he is also hidden there, concealed in the inner sanctum, or in rituals that only the initiated can decipher. Churches, mosques and temples still convey this feeling, even to the one who enters them in unbelief. What exactly is its source – its deep source in the human psyche, that is, rather than in myths and stories? The answer is touched on by St Paul, in 1 Cor. 6.19: 'Do you not know that your body is a temple of the Holy Spirit, who is in you, whom you have received from God?'

The human body is the temple of the soul, the place where the other is both present and hidden, protected from me but nevertheless revealed when the right words are uttered and the right gestures made. 'There is but one temple in the world,' wrote Novalis (*Hymns to the Night*), 'and that is the body of man ... We touch Heaven when we lay hand on a human body.' In everyday life we don't see things in quite that way. The busy transactions of work, play and marketplace are like the fussy to-ings and fro-ings of priests before the altar. They take attention away from the real presence, which demands purifying rites if it is to be revealed to us. But in the intimacy of love, anger or desire I encounter the other as *haunted by himself*. I look *into* him and he becomes a presence that I sense but which flees from my attempts to conjure it, until the right look or word or touch brings it suddenly to rest and face to face with me. It is on this experience that we draw, I think, when we respond to the temple as a shrine. God is a real presence in his temple, as I am in my body, even if 'reserved', as in the 'reserved sacrament' of the Catholic Church.

In traditional Japanese society, whose balletic contours have been immortalized in prints and plays, we see people treating each other in this special and 'reserved' way. Each person on the Noh stage is standing in a sacred space: the space consecrated to the I. And the eyes burn in that space like the lamp on the altar, even when they burn behind a mask. The sanctity of the person is a human universal, and when we bow before the other, even when we reach out to shake his hand, we display our recognition that the space which he occupies cannot be violated, that a gesture of submission and acquiescence is needed, in order to acknowledge his sacred right to be present just there, where his body is. For the same reason many ways of attacking people are desecrations – negative acknowledgements of the sacred nature of the body. That is why Shakespeare, in order to complete the desecration that is set in motion by Lear's failure to see the true eye of love, brings the play to a turning point with the tearing out of Gloucester's eyes. This violation of the temple presages the final violation, which leaves Cordelia dead, her father holding a feather before her face, in the vain hope that the soul still breathes from it.

The parallel between the body and the temple influences the forms of sacred architecture. Like the human being, the temple stands upright. It is not a single monolith any more than the human body is a continuous solid. It is the exfoliation of a generative code, contained within the primary unit of the column, the dimensions of which provide the scalar measure for the entire building. The generative nature of temple architecture is a profoundly *spiritualizing* feature of it. Everywhere the stone bears the mark of a shaping intention. Elements are fitted together in the relationship that Alberti described as *concinnitas* – which means the apt correspondence of part to part, the ability of one detail to give a clear visual answer to the 'why?' posed by another.[3] A temple is not simply a work of load-bearing stone. The column is carved, fluted, adorned with plinth and capital, crowned by a frieze or an arch or joined in heavenly vaults where stone achieves the lightness of the sky. Through mouldings and decorative details the stone is filled with shadow, acquires an appearance of crystallized light, translucent, as the face is translucent, to the spirit within (Figure 13).

In a manuscript note left by the architect Sir John Soane we read that 'mouldings are as essential and important to

3. *De re aedificatoria*, 1452, trans. Leoni, 1726.

Figure 13. Federal Hall, New York.

the architect as colours to the painter'.[4] Soane was a classical architect, and one of the greatest. But his observation applies to all the styles that have been associated with the stone temple. The upright column, embellished by vault or archi-trave, and enlivened by mouldings, provides the *lingua franca* of sacred architecture from the ancient Middle East and Mediterranean to the present day. And the outward features of temple architecture were borrowed and normalized by the vernacular styles with which our towns and cities were built.[5] Our towns are home to the people who live in them in part because their buildings perpetuate the experience of the face. This we see in Figure 14, a simple street from the town of Whitby, in which the posture of the temple, and the worn

4. Sir John Soane's Museum Archives 1/164/6. Fol. [1]. I owe this reference to David Watkin.
5. I have defended this point in *The Classical Vernacular*, Manchester, Carcanet Press, 1992.

Figure 14. Street in Whitby.

residue of ancient forms and mouldings, endow each unpretentious building with a face, and raise the lamp above the street like a blessing. People are hurt by the faceless blocks that now intrude into such streets not simply because they dislike the style or have yet to become accustomed to it, but because the connection with the tradition of temple architecture has been finally severed. Columnar order, mouldings, façade, and the delicate stitching of the building to the street below and the sky above – all these things are now being discarded. And the result gives rise to a peculiar feeling of desolation, which is the normal, but now widely misunderstood, response to an act of desecration.

Sacred places are the first places to be destroyed by invaders and iconoclasts, for whom nothing is more offensive than the enemy's gods. And we should recognize that much of the destruction of our environment today is *deliberate*, the result of a willed assault on old and despised forms of tranquillity. For there are two broad approaches to building: the way of settlement, and the way of disruption. Often when we settle we fit our lives into an existing and already consecrated pattern, strive to inherit the order established by those who have come before us, and to honour the spirit of the place: in this sense, as Heidegger points out in an important essay, to build is to dwell.[6] But the iconoclast seeks to replace old gods with new, to disenchant the landscape and to mark the place with signs of his defiance. This iconoclastic spirit can be seen in a great many modern projects – not only in the faceless curtain walls of the new building types, but in the bleak intrusive wind farms that are eating up the landscape, or in the postmodern blemishes deliberately inserted into settled urban schemes by architects like Daniel Libeskind and Thom Mayne.

The environmental movement began in Britain as a reaction to the industrial revolution and in America as a lament for the disappearing wilderness. In both places writers and activists began to portray the Earth as a quasi-animate being, to whom we could relate as pagans related to their gods. John Muir's plea for the Yosemite valley, like Ruskin's campaign to save the Lakelands of England, was on behalf of a place judged to be sacred – a place whose value could therefore never be captured by the calculus of cost and benefit. James Lovelock's more recent 'Gaia hypothesis' is an attempt to translate that idea into the language of science.[7] From the point of view of philosophy, however, the Gaia hypothesis misses what is really at stake. There is something left out of every scientific account of our relation to our surroundings, and that is the I to You

6. Martin Heidegger, 'Building, Dwelling, Thinking', in *Poetry, Language, Thought*, trans. Albert Hofstadter, New York, Harper Colophon, 1971.
7. James Lovelock, *Gaia: A New Look at Life on Earth*, 1979, third edn, Oxford, OUP, 2000.

encounter, and the sense of responsibility that it precipitates. This is what our forebears built into their temples, and it is why temples are both sacred places and candidates for desecration. But what could it possibly mean to say that the earth itself could be encountered in such a way?

In the ninth of the *Duino Elegies*, Rilke tries to answer that question. He seeks the subjectivity of the earth, and discovers it in *us* – it is we who have the task of translating into consciousness the things that surround us, and so rescuing them from the world of getting and spending:

Erde, ist es nicht dies, was du willst: *unsichtbar*
in uns erstehn? – Ist es dein Traum nicht,
einmal unsichtbar zu sein? Erde! unsichtbar!
Was, wenn Verwandlung nicht, ist dein drängender Auftrag?
Erde, du liebe, ich will. Oh glaub, es bedürfte
nicht deiner Frühlinge mehr, mich dir zu gewinnen, – einer,
ach, ein einziger ist schon dem Blute zu viel.[8]

In these lines Rilke attempts to re-consecrate the earth by dissolving it, so to speak, in his first person perspective. The poet repudiated every kind of transcendental faith and believed that there is no after life, but only this one life on earth, which we can waste or fulfil as we choose. But he also believed that life is sacred, as are all the beings that we encounter in the course of it. He believed in the God within who is a God of subjectivity, a God as lonely and vulnerable as the poet who harbours him, but who is able to reach out and enchant the poet's world. Rilke's purpose in the *Duino Elegies* was to draw on the raw material from which every

8. Earth, isn't this what you want: *invisibly* to arise in us? Is it not your dream to be some day invisible? Earth! Invisible! What, if not transformation, is your insistent demand? Earth, dear one, I will! Oh believe me, it needs no more of your spring times to win me over. One, just one, is already too much for my blood.

experience of the sacred is derived – namely the first person experience of embodiment – and to use it to build a path out of nihilism. The earth is not just a heap of objects; it has its own subjectivity, and it achieves this subjectivity in me.

The concerns expressed by environmentalists have arisen largely in opposition to the habit of seeing all value in instrumental terms. People have treated the earth and their surroundings as things to be *used*, and when their use is exhausted to be thrown away, thereafter to be washed into one of those sinks, like the oceans and the atmosphere, which we have no need to clean. But the sinks are finite, our waste accumulates forever, and the oceans and the atmosphere have had enough of us. A platform of plastic waste twice the size of Texas reportedly swirls in the Pacific Ocean; green house gases build up in the atmosphere, raising the temperature of the earth and threatening everything that we know and need. And all around us we see the residue of our gluttony as, in the words of William Empson, 'Slowly the poison the whole bloodstream fills:/ It is the waste, the waste remains and kills.'

When governments address the problem they construe it in fiscal terms, considering the economic costs of our negligence and the economic costs of repairing it. The British government commissioned a report from Sir Nicholas Stern to consider 'the economic costs of climate change' and of the policies needed to correct it. And this report has served as the basis for almost all the arguments in the political arena ever since – so making it seem as though the earth and our environment are to be assessed purely in instrumental terms, and without any consideration for their intrinsic value.[9] This triumph of instrumental reasoning, which describes things with a value as things with a price, is perhaps inevitable. But it

9. Sir Nicholas Stern, *The Economics of Climate Change*, Cambridge, CUP, 2007. See the devastating critique of the instrumental approach to the environment by Mark Sagoff, *Price, Principle and the Environment*, Cambridge, CUP, 2004.

is also one of the features of the modern world against which the environmentalists are, or ought to be, in rebellion. The environmental problem arises because we have treated the earth as an object and an instrument, in something like the way that we have treated the human being as an object and an instrument. And surely it is not unrealistic to connect the two developments. We have fallen into the habit of seeing everything, ourselves included, as a thing to be used and consumed, and this is rightly called a fall. Indeed, this is what the 'fall of man' consists in. Eating the forbidden fruit means believing that it is for *us* to define the distinction between good and evil. We then rewrite the distinction in purely human terms: good and evil become benefit and cost, so that nothing is holy, nothing is consecrated, nothing is rescued from barter and exchange. We deal with the world by pricing it. Things that are valued only for their use can then be compared with, exchanged against, and sold for other things of the same kind. They can be consumed, depleted and thrown away, by the person who nevertheless acknowledges the only value that they have, which is the cost of a replacement. That is what we now do to each other and to the earth. Yet the earth is irreplaceable, just as we are.

The sense of the sacred puts a brake upon that instrumental attitude. Before a sacred place or artefact I stand back in a posture of respect. This bit of the world, I believe, is inviolable. I could damage it, and maybe I won't be punished for doing so. But it speaks to me, and tells me to stay my hand. Just as the subject appears in the human face, and lays before the assassin and the abuser the absolute 'no', so does an observing, questing, interrogating 'I' appear in the sacred place, and command us to respect it.

Sceptics will say that that is just figurative talk, a lapse into what Ruskin called the 'pathetic fallacy'.[10] They will argue that

10. *Modern Painters*, Part IV, Chapter 13.

I am expressing subjective emotions that have no objective correlate in the things on which they are projected. It is our way of *treating* places and artefacts that makes them sacred, and our decision to do so is invariably rescinded in time.

Two points need to be made in reply. The first is that the experience of the sacred is inter-personal. Only creatures with 'I' thoughts can see the world in this way, and their doing so depends upon a kind of inter-personal readiness, a willingness to find meanings and reasons, even in things that have no eyes to look at them and no mouth to speak. That is what Alberti meant by the striving for *concinnitas*. True architects do not subdue their material to some external purpose; they *converse* with it, allowing the material to interrogate the space in which they build. The anthropologist might say that the experience of the sacred is a residue of primitive animism. I would counter by saying that animism is not a primitive thing, but a legitimate extension of our sense of accountability. Because we are subjects the world looks back at us

Figure 15. Sunset Boulevard, Los Angeles.

with a questioning regard, and we respond by organizing and conceptualizing it in other ways than those endorsed by science. The world as we live it is not the world as science explains it, any more than the smile of the Mona Lisa is a smear of pigments on a canvas. But this lived world is as real as the Mona Lisa's smile.

The second point is that the experience of sacred things is one special case of a more general capacity to find meaning and moral refreshment in the things of this world. Creatures with 'I' thoughts have a relation to their surroundings that is unlike that of an animal to its habitat. The question 'why am I here?', which is a constant refrain in the life of the rational being, flips into the question 'why is *here* here?' – in other words, what is the significance for me, of the fact that this thing, this place, this *Umwelt* that I confront *is* the thing that I confront? This recalls Gertrude Stein's dismissal of small-town America: 'there is no *there* there'. Stein showed a true insight into our relation with the earth. Sometimes there is nothing there; and sometimes it is *we* who make that nothingness, by defacing the world, as in the junk city left in its wake by the motor car.[11]

Figure 15 shows a part of Sunset Boulevard, Los Angeles, a pile of man-made junk in which, here and there, old attempts at dwelling can be discerned, but in which everything has the air of something provisional and discarded. Contrast the jumbled backwater canal from Venice in Figure 16. Why is this not junk, and why is it a place of dwelling? Look at the details, and you will soon find, in the side-by-sideness of the windows, in their stone surrounds and the pilasters of the door, in the lipped moulding along the canal and the stone arch of the bridge, in every crumbling, peeling element some

11. See James Howard Kunstler, *The Geography of Nowhere: The Rise and Decline of America's Man-Made Landscape*, New York, Free Press, 1993, and follow the 'Eyesore of the Month' tab on Kunstler's web-site.

Figure 16. Canal in Venice.

reminiscence of the temple and its enchanted order. This canal is transparently lived in and every detail has a use: but no detail was *dictated* by its use, so that a kind of joyful redundancy inhabits each façade. Such examples help us to understand what was lost when the modernist vernacular took over, and the city of slabs replaced the city of columns. Le Corbusier aptly introduced the modernist idiom with the dictum that 'a house is a machine for living in': in other words, my home is not a subject but an object – a place without a face.

We find ourselves here in philosophical territory that was mapped out by Kant in the *Critique of Judgement*. The topic of the first part of that book is the judgement of beauty – a judgement that we all make, and which we need to make, Kant believed, if we are to achieve a full understanding of the world and of our own rational capacities. Beauty resides in appearances, but appearances are also realities, and things that we share. Our interest in appearances stems from the desire to be at home in our surroundings, and to find inscribed in the world of objects some record of our personal concerns. Oscar Wilde remarked that it is only a shallow person who does not judge by appearances; I would add that judging by appearances is what makes persons possible. It is in the world of appearances that we become what we truly are, and one proof of this is the human face – the place in which the human subject comes into view, and readies itself for others.

The *Critique of Pure Reason* established that appearances are not the passively received 'impressions' of the empiricist myth, but the products of a profound interaction between subject and object, by which we impose form and order on the input received through our senses. In our everyday inter-action with the world the objects of experience come before us as 'to be known' or 'to be used'. But there is another posture open to us, in which appearances are ordered as objects to be contemplated. In the experience of the beautiful we take the world into consciousness, and let it float there. To put it another way: we savour the world, as something *given*, and not just as something received. This is not like the savouring of a taste or a smell: it involves a reflective study of meanings, and an attempt to find the human significance of the things that appear before us, *as* they appear. This savouring of impressions leads of its own accord to a critical attitude, and to reason-governed choices. I measure the object observed against the subject observing it and put both in question. This happens when I attend a drama, and respond to the action on stage as though living through it, or when I sit in a tranquil landscape and allow the appearance to seep through my feelings and to become part of me.

In aesthetic attention I am enjoying objects for their own sake, and even if their utility is part of what they mean to me (as when I admire a fine building or a beautiful plough-share) it is not by using them that I appreciate their aesthetic value. How exactly to express the point is one of the deep

and difficult questions of philosophy. Let us simply say that
aesthetic values are intrinsic values, and that when I find
beauty in some object it is because I am seeing it as an end
in itself and not only as a means. And its intrinsic meaning
for me lies in its presented form, its way of coming before my
perception, so as to challenge me in the here and now. That
way of encountering objects in the world is importantly like
my way of seeing persons, when they stand before me face to
face and I recognize that I am accountable to them and they
to me. In the aesthetic experience we have something like
a face-to-face encounter with the world itself, and with the
things that it contains, just as we have in the experience of
sacred things and sacred places.[12]

Although, by definition, intrinsic values cannot be translated into utilitarian values, this does not mean that they
have no utility. Consider friendship. Your friend is valuable
to you as the thing that he is. To treat him as a means – to
use him for your purposes – is to undo the friendship. And
yet friends are useful: they provide help in times of need, and
they amplify the joys of daily living. Friendship is supremely
useful, so long as we do not think of it as useful. Likewise
with the environment. It is not that the economists are wrong
to think that the environment is useful to us, or that the costs
and benefits can be calculated and weighed in the balance. It
is that the most important benefits come to us only when we
do not weigh them in the balance. We gain the benefits of the
earth when we cease to aim for them. And that is the role of
beauty, which comes before the vandal and the abuser as the
face of the victim before the would-be assassin. It utters a
quiet but absolute 'no' that can be overridden by violence, but
not removed by calculation. And often this 'no' is received as
a face-to-face challenge – as though the object were speaking

---

12. For further expansion of this theme, see Roger Scruton, *Beauty: A Very Short
     Introduction*, Oxford, OUP, 2009.

to the spectator, I to you. The monk who burned down the famous temple of the Golden Pavilion at Kyoto – the greatest treasure of Japanese architecture – said that he set fire to it because it was so beautiful, and its beauty was a judgement against himself.[13] Surely an inter-personal response, if ever there was one.

This leads me to a very important observation, which is that beauty can be defaced, and where there is aesthetic value there is also the possibility of desecration. I discussed the desire to deface in connection with human sexual experience. A similar desire is present in our confrontation with our surroundings. Beauty, order and the home create demands. They are to be respected, and we feel judged by them, as we are judged by other subjects. Hence there arises a desire to take revenge, to wipe away the knowing smile with which they look on our imperfections. The beautiful object demands to be contemplated, but not consumed. And in a world of instrumental values this demand may be received as a rebuke. The habit of waste and litter is in part a response to this. Places where order and beauty can enter our world and make a difference are privatized, so as to become 'me' occasions, and to lose the aspect of dialogue in which their beauty resides.

Two aspects of popular culture illustrate the 'me' attitude, and the damage that it wreaks on public space: graffiti and fast food. Graffiti are acts of aggression against the public realm, ways of 'defacing' it. Often they involve caricatures of writing by people who are taking their revenge on the skill which, above all others, symbolizes the act of inter-personal communication. In most cases the graffiti vandal is offended by the sight of a settled place, a place that excludes him since he does not and cannot belong. He belongs not to a place but

13. The episode has been brilliantly portrayed in a novel by Yukio Mishima, *The Temple of the Golden Pavilion*, 1956, trans. Ivan Morris, New York, Alfred A. Knopf, 1959.

to the nomadic gang that is passing through, angered by the sight of others' settlement.

Something similar should be said about fast food. This does not merely wipe out the place (the shared meal) in which aesthetic values enter daily life and order it, but also leaves a trail of packaging and waste across the surface of the world. It desecrates townscapes and landscapes with childish logos, of a kind that reinforce the message that eating takes place *outside* society, in places to which we return from the world of obligations as infants return to the breast. If you had been looking for a way to deface our world and close up the avenue to meaning, you could hardly have found a more effective one.

The subject of aesthetics took off when Kant and Hume simultaneously recognized (though on very different grounds) that aesthetic enjoyment involves a judgement. It is founded in a sense of the rightness of the object that I enjoy, as it is presented to my attention. Kant and Hume wrote in this connection of the 'judgement of taste'. That eighteenth-century way of expressing the point is misleading, since the word 'taste' is now used to describe the most arbitrary of our preferences in food and drink. The point is better expressed in terms of the normative character of aesthetic choices. Our ordinary aesthetic judgements concern what is right and wrong, what fits and harmonizes, what looks and sounds appropriate. Dressing for a party, laying a table, decorating a room and so on, are all aimed at the *right* appearance, and the pleasure taken is inseparable from the judgement that the thing looks as it should. There is an *internal* relation here, between preference and judgement. Hence, whether we like it or not (and most people don't like it) we become answerable to other rational beings for our aesthetic choices. Through these choices we are creating presences in the world of others; and what they think of the result is part of how it matters both to them and to us. This is not to say that we can *find* reasons for our choices, still less that we can find *justifying* reasons. But we are in some sense committed to the existence of those reasons, and the art of criticism consists in discovering paths to them.

Neither Kant nor Hume came up with an argument that could really underpin this search for 'the standard of taste', though both had interesting and far-reaching things to say about it. But the phenomenon appears less mysterious, I believe, if we see it as arising from the I–You relationship, and from our intrinsic tendency towards accountability. Aesthetic judgement is a fundamental element in the posture described by the German romantics as *Heimkehr* – the turning for home. The love of beauty is founded in the need for settlement, for a place that we share, where, as Hölderlin puts it,

Alles scheinet vertraut, der vorübereilende Gruß auch
Scheint von Freunden, es scheint jegliche Miene verwandt ...

'all seems familiar, even the casual greeting seems like a friend's, and every face belongs' ('*Heimkunft*' – Homecoming). In designing our surroundings we are bringing them within the sphere of accountability to others and theirs to us. And in that sense we are providing the world with a face. We deface the world when we scribble 'me' all over it, and invite others to do the same. Beauty is the face of the community, and ugliness the attack on that face by the solipsist and the scavenger.

It is for this reason that thinkers and artists of the Enlightenment turned to natural beauty to fill the God-shaped hole in their worldview. The Romantic Movement was a movement of unsettled souls in search of settlement, and such is the theme of Caspar David Friedrich's paintings, in which man and nature stand face to face, in a kind of yearning alienation (Figure 17). In the Romantic landscape the beautiful replaces the sacred as the source of meaning. God once promised a home, and urged us to consecrate it

Figure 17. Friedrich: Wanderer Above a Sea of Fog.

in his name. But the path to that home became overgrown, and the promise unbelievable. The Romantics were making another path: the path of 'aesthetic education'.[14] Beauty, for them, was a promise – the promise of community, even if only an imagined community that has yet to find a place on earth. They replaced the sacred with the beautiful, without noticing that this is what they had done. And we should find nothing strange in this, once we recognize that both conceptions arise from a single metaphysical source, which is the I–You relation, extended from persons to things.

Beautiful nature does not merely occur, however: it is usually *built*, and even when understood as wholly 'natural' is experienced in terms of the life-possibilities that it offers. That was true of the American wilderness that Thoreau, Emerson and Muir wished to protect from human predation. For the native Americans the landscape had in fact been a managed home, whose every contour bore witness to the

14. See Friedrich von Schiller, *Letters upon the Aesthetic Education of Man*, trans. E. Wilkinson and L. A. Willoughby, Oxford, Clarendon Press, 1967.

life-style that the white man had extinguished. The romantic poets and painters of the new America were re-configuring the landscape as wilderness, and their conception of its beauty was the by-product of another form of settlement than the one destroyed. It is not that the Romantics found beauty in nature: it is rather that they created and transfigured nature through the pursuit of beauty, which is the search for home.

We shape our surroundings as a home by farming, by building, by arranging the world. Aesthetic values govern every form of settlement, and it is the nomads, those 'passing through', who acknowledge no responsibility for the way things appear around them. The face of nature, as we see it in the great landscape paintings of Constable and Crome, of Courbet and Corot, is a face *turned towards us,* giving and receiving both frowns and smiles. And later artists showed another kind of expression, called forth onto the face of nature by the urgent desire to find what is *really there*, regardless of all the myths and stories. In the paintings of Van Gogh trees, flowers, orchards, fields and buildings break open to the artist's brush, in something like the way that a human face can break open in response to a smile, to reveal an intense inner life and an affirmation of being. Throughout the nineteenth century artists, poets and composers were in this way exploring and imploring the face of nature, eager for a direct and I-to-I encounter. The desire to perpetuate this face and to save it from unnecessary blemishes motivated the environmental movement, which was (in its origins, at least) the political expression of a profoundly Romantic sensibility.

In England the movement led to the foundation of the National Trust by Octavia Hill and others in 1895. Octavia Hill was a follower of Ruskin, and like him she held that natural beauty belongs to everyone. By respecting and conserving it, she believed, we maintain the face that forbids the destroyer. Commendable though such initiatives may be, they have a tendency to concentrate on the accumulated inheritance of buildings, landscapes and townscapes, without regard to the human life that endowed them with their soul. The parks and houses preserved by the National Trust owe their beauty to patterns of ownership that the Trust itself destroys. The beauty of such things may be a common asset; but it was produced by private ownership, and it is ownership that retrieves our towns and parks from the menacing nothingness of slab architecture – the kind of architecture exemplified by the Soviet 'Monotowns', built around a single production line and many now crumbling wastelands of prefabricated junk. The temple is our paradigm, because although not owned by any human being, it is owned by God, whose home it is. And the rest of the townscape grows from private attempts to embellish the home, using the soul-speech of the temple in the doorways, architraves and window-surrounds that frame the life within.

The 'ensoulling' of the world through ownership is conveyed in the Old Testament story of God's first gift to man, the Garden of Eden. A garden is a cultivated place, a place transformed by aesthetic choices, a place that bears the mark of human labour and human desire. It is the very image of the process that Locke believed to be the foundation of private property: the 'mixing' of labour with the things of the earth.[15] Hence gardens have their own distinctive phenomenology, in which nature is taken up, tamed and marked by human interest. A garden is not an open space like a landscape, but a surrounding space. And that which grows and stands in it, grows and stands *around* the observer. A tree in a garden is not like a tree in a forest or a field. It is not simply there, growing accidentally from some scattered seed. It was planted there, and as a result it stands and watches the observer, as the observer in turn stands and watches the tree. And

15. See the *Second Treatise of Civil Government*.

although it does not move, the tree converses with those who walk beneath it and who look up through its branches to the sky. Trees standing in a garden are standing between the human world and the realm of pure nature. Indeed, there is a phenomenological 'between-ness' that infects all our ordinary ways of enjoying a garden. This experience feeds into our understanding of architectural forms and decorations, as things designed to conquer space and enclose it, to capture it from nature and to present it as *ours*.

A public space, therefore, is not an unowned space, but one in which the many spheres of ownership come to a negotiated boundary. This boundary may be a street, a sequence of façades, or a sky-line. It represents the side-by-side settlement of private owners, and the way of life that they share. Hence when the boundary is punctured or stolen by some private interest we react to this as a desecration. This is especially true in cities, which have been, and to a certain extent still are, sacred places, whose contours record a continuous dialogue over centuries between 'neighbours' – those who 'build nearby', to give the Anglo-Saxon etymology of the word. The culture of consumption sweeps across them like a tornado, scattering in its wake the doll-like images of advertising models, which wash up across the buildings and hide them from view, as in the bill-board- and digital-image-covered streets of today's Bucharest, a city once described as 'the Paris of the East' (Figure 18).

Here we encounter an interesting paradox, which is that nothing has so great a power to deface as the face. The realistic presentation of a human face always risks uglifying the building on which it is displayed. The human form can be represented on a façade in sculpted figures, busts and caryatids without disturbing the architectural order: but that is because such details incorporate the figure into the architecture, subdue its pre-eminent claim to our attention, and enable us to abstract from the immediacy and the addictive excess to which the

Figure 18. Uniri Square, Bucharest.

lifelike images of our kind may tempt us. By contrast hoardings and bill-boards desecrate the public spaces that contain them, and never more so than when a human face appears in them, launching its urgent appeal to be the centre of attention.

Some light is cast on this paradox by the Jewish and Muslim attitude to idolatry. The second commandment does not merely forbid 'graven images' purporting to represent God. It forbids 'any likeness of any thing that is in Heaven above, or that is in the earth beneath, or that is in the water under the earth'. A *hadith* of Muhammad forbids pictures in the home, telling us that whoever makes a picture will not only be punished on the Last Day, but will be forced to give life to the thing that he has created.[16]

These strange-seeming interdictions remain in force, as we know not only from the recent controversy over cartoon images of the Prophet, but also from the long tradition of

16. *Sahih Buhari*, vol. 4, Book 54, Number 447.

Islamic art and carpet-weaving, in which figurative elements are avoided, or else deliberately 'geometrized' and thereby deprived of their *nafs* or 'soul'. In Christian culture too image-making has been frequently contentious, with spells of iconoclasm alternating with periods of devout religious imagery, as in ancient Byzantium and in post-medieval Europe. In a wide-ranging study the French philosopher Alain Besançon has argued that the fear and suspicion of images has influenced the development of religion and philosophy throughout recorded history, and has not disappeared merely because we are now surrounded and distracted by images on every side and at every moment of the day.[17] Indeed, much of what disturbs us in our current predicament is what disturbed the theologians of Islam: namely, that the 'graven image', which begins as a representation, soon becomes a substitute. And substitutes corrupt the feelings that they invite, in the way that idols corrupt worship, and porn corrupts desire. For substitutes invite easy and mechanical responses. They short-circuit the costly process whereby we form real relationships, and put mechanical and addictive reflexes in their place. The idol does not represent God: it defaces him.

The emotional disorder involved in this is the theme of Poussin's painting of the *Golden Calf* (Figure 19). The foreground is dominated by the calf, raised on its pedestal. The idol is a glowing surrogate, life-like but dead, with the emphatic deadness of metal. Aaron gestures with priestly cunning to his creation, while the people, drunk, helpless and in the grip of collective delusion, dance brainlessly around this thing less sacred than themselves. In focusing on the calf their emotions are also out of focus – bewildered, diseased, gyrating in a void. In the distance, barely visible, is the figure of Moses, descending from Mount Sinai with the tables of

17. Alain Besançon, *L'image interdite: une histoire intellectuelle de l'iconoclasme*, Paris, Gallimard, 2000.

Figure 19. Nicolas Poussin: The Golden Calf.

the law: the abstract decrees of an abstract God, who can be understood through no earthly image but only through law. Moses casts the stone tablets to the ground, destroying thereby not the law but its earthly record. The vastness of Aaron, his face irradiated by a specious and self-satisfied calm, contrasts with the smallness and fragility of Moses, his body collapsed in anger, wordless in the face of willing servitude, as he was later to be portrayed by Schoenberg in his great unfinished opera on this theme.

Underlying Poussin's vision is a contrast between the active work of the intellect, which points to a God beyond the sensory world, and the passive force of fantasy, which creates its own god out of sensory desires. There is also a contrast between two kinds of authority: one based on law, the other on charisma. The effort of religion, Poussin shows, is to lift the human soul from fantasy images and mortal appetites, and direct it towards a real relation with a transcendental God. But this effort is difficult, and cannot succeed without the 'real presence' that Moses alone had encountered. Looking for the face of God, the people turn to a surrogate. Their idolatry becomes an *obstacle* to religion, rather than a form of it. It involves perverting from their true course the emotions, thoughts and actions that are due to God.

To the devout Muslim even Poussin's painting is a form of idolatry – a 'likeness' which, in aping the creative power, dilutes the authority of God. Christians of a puritan persuasion have destroyed statues, paintings, stained glass and any other object which has served the religious uses of simple people, believing that these too are idols, and that in destroying them they do the work of God. There is, indeed, a tradition within Protestantism that sees organized religion itself as a kind of idolatry – which repudiates all ceremonies, texts and liturgical words as human products, and finds holiness in one thing alone, which is the inner relation to a transcendental God. This way of thinking can be taken to paradoxical extremes. In the bleak theology of Karl Barth, for example, there is nothing to be known of God except that he is unknowable, concealed behind every image, every story, every *idea* even, which purports to reveal him. The path of religion is the *via negativa* of Avicenna and Maimonides, that leads away from all worldly thoughts and things. Worship then becomes a perpetually renewed iconoclasm, aimed at the entire human world.

For Poussin idolatry involves a loss of the soul. The Israelites are dancing with formless movements round and round, their faces wreathed in idiot smiles, their emotions herd-like and confused. They are no longer moral beings, answerable to the law, but animals, driven by collective instincts that acknowledge no law but only the magic of the enchanter Aaron.

The contrast here is not with the Barthian Protestant, wordlessly contemplating his unknowable God, nor even with Schoenberg's equally wordless Moses. The contrast is with the ordinary believer, who worships God in his own way, recognizing that worship involves obedience, and attaching his worship to the ethical life. Such a believer might well make use of images and intermediaries. Those who worship before the crucifix or the statue of the Blessed Virgin are not worshipping the object, but the holy person that it represents. There are many cases here, and to describe them all as idolatry is to miss the important distinctions – in particular, the distinction between a representation and a surrogate, and between the focus of a feeling and its object.

By focusing on the face we feed our love and take delight in it. By focusing on bodily functions we sully love and deprive it of its ethical authority. And that is the contrast that Poussin puts before us. The Israelites have fixed their gaze on a human creation, and so undermined the God-ward intentionality of worship. Their worship has been voided of its inter-personal significance and they are adrift, directionless, and bewildered. For Poussin it is not God who is threatened by idolatry but man: idolatry is literally soul-destroying. And in the drunkenness of the Israelites Poussin has captured the essentially addictive nature of the idolatrous response: its nature as a 'short-circuit' to an empty reward.

The conflict over idolatry helps us to understand what is at stake in environmental questions today. Lamentations over the trashing of the urban landscape have taken an aesthetic form not because the issue concerns 'a matter of taste', which therefore lies beyond any political resolution, but because the issue concerns a matter of soul. The debates around modernism and post-modernism, around the New Urbanism and the dominion of the 'starchitects' are about something of the first importance to all of us, which is the face of the world. And we will understand them best if we return to the original guidance given to Moses.

God's instructions were to build his temple around its

pillars. As I have already suggested, it is not too fanciful to connect the pillars of the temple with the classical Orders – the column-based rules for organizing the outward aspect of buildings, which provided a kind of generative grammar of the meaningful façade. The classical orders, so understood, provided the core discipline of city architecture in the Western tradition, from antiquity until the eve of the First World War – in other words, from the birth of our civilization to its first attempt at suicide.

As sacred places, cities must begin from an act of consecration. Consecration is something we do – presenting a thing for divine endorsement. It is the theme of all those rites of passage whereby communities renew themselves. And it is the beginning of any building that is to be permanent – any building in which settlement is the goal. The secret of the classical tradition is that it takes the act of consecration and generalizes it. The upright posture of the column, in which the building stands before me, I to You, is endowed with a face, by the division into sections, and by the elaboration of mouldings and transitions. Our ability to endow buildings with faces is like our ability to see character in a theatrical mask. By facing a building we conjure a face in it, and by silently addressing it we allow the building to address us in its turn. This 'facing' of a building stands to the defacing by a bill-board as real devotion stands to idolatry.

From the conception of the temple, permeable to the city yet sacred and removed from it, came that of the colonnade, and thence of the single column as the unit of meaning. The Orders endow the architectural unit with maximum sacred power, while laying down a law for the building as a whole. They also embody immensely sophisticated solutions to the problems of design: how to turn corners; how to present a single aspect from many points of view; how to translate ideas of strength, variety and permanence into a thousand plans and façades.

The Roman building types – arch, aedicule, engaged column, pilaster, vault and dome – can all be seen as attempts to retain the sacred presence of the column, in all the uses of civic life. In them we see the interpenetration of the sacred and the secular, and thus the sanctifying of the human community and the humanizing of the divine. That is the source of their appeal and the reason for their durability. With the Roman building types began the true history of Western architecture: which is the history of the *implied Order*. This is the order contained in the pattern-books, and preserved in cornices, window surrounds, string courses and door frames, in chimneys and railings, in all our city streets before the twentieth century (see again Figures 13 and 14).

Although it is possible to exaggerate the difference between the classical temple and the Gothic church, this at least should always be remembered: that the classical temple marks out an inner sanctum in the space of our world, while the Gothic cathedral is the gateway to another space, potentially infinite, and outside the sphere of daily life. We pass through its doors into a heavenly realm, stretching upwards and outwards forever, and its never-ending movement invites us to a divine discontent with earthly things. Because its sacred meaning is not of this world, its forms lend themselves only precariously to domestic and civil uses, and the Gothic vernacular has never been more than a passing dream – the dream of a Pugin, who longed to re-capture the world of Christian obedience in an age of dwindling faith. The Gothic revival produced dreamscapes and fairyland castles – not the face of God in the world of men, but a divine mirage, refracted from the undiscovered country beyond the edge of the world.

The classical forms survived the secularizing forces of modernity, and have even been used to give those forces architectural expression. Indeed, the principle of the implied Order helped to ease us into the secular world, by retaining the calm and unobtrusive background to our 'experiments

in living'. There the Orders stand, affirming what is sempi-
ternal in the midst of change, and endorsing our sense that
we *belong* where we are, and belong as a community. They
are the visible licence to dwell, the affirmation of our right of
occupation, and the reminder that we belong to a community
not of the living only, but of the dead and the unborn. That
is the secret of their civility, which is more than politeness –
being rather a kind of piety, and a consecration of the place
where they stand.

As the Orders make clear, the true discipline of form
emphasizes the vertical line. The art of design is to a great
extent the art of vertical accumulation, of placing one thing
above another, so as to create an order which can be spread
rhythmically from side to side, as in the colonnade or the
terraced street.

To endow a façade with vertical order we must exploit
light, shade and climate, we must divide the wall space, and
emphasize apertures. In other words we must use mouldings.
In the early years of the skyscraper tall buildings were
conceived like the Chrysler building in New York, as exultant
fingers pointing to the sky. The real ugliness came later,
when the skyscraper was stripped of all those lines, shadows
and curlicues that were the source of its life and gaiety.
Without mouldings no space is articulate. Edges become
blades; buildings lose their crowns and walls their direction
(since movement sideways has the same visual emphasis
as movement up and down). Windows and doors either
disappear entirely or lose their character as aedicules and
become mere holes in the wall. No part is framed, marked off,
emphasized or softened. Everything is sheer, stark, uncom-
promising, cold. Without mouldings we no longer build with
light and shade but with the poured plastic forms of gadgets
– objects without orientation, and with no place of their own.

Hence, lacking that kind of vertical order, modern high-rise
buildings are conceived as stacks of horizontal layers, piled

one on the other and requiring no design other than the ground plan, as in Mies van der Rohe's much admired Seagram building of 1958, the model for a thousand steel and glass office blocks since constructed all around the world. Mies's building provides the template for an architecture generated not from the vertical column and the language of shadow, but from the horizontal ground plan. The result can be as tall as you like – as tall as the Seagram building – but it will never have a vertical posture, and never meet you face to face. What should have been a face is merely the edge of the plan.

In such a building, boundaries and units of significance are muted or absent. There are no windows; no decorated corners; no places from which the building looks out at passers by. It is a sealed box, with translucent walls – but made of glass and bronze in alternating strips. It reminds you of those people who appear in company wearing dark glasses behind which, you are forced to think, is no self, since self exists only as recognized by others. Such people hide the I from eyes, since eyes are judges.

A building constructed on the Seagram principle exists on a constant diet of energy – to heat it in winter, and to cool it in summer. Moreover, since it is sealed from the outer air, it requires yet more energy to circulate air around its interior, and that air gradually becomes home to the many diseases that are brought in by the workforce, so that the building itself becomes sick. Yet the Seagram template has been followed for half a century – without the bronze, and with a steel frame and curtain wall of glass or concrete panels. It is the existence of this style of architecture, more than any other cause, that has led to the desertification of downtown America. Such buildings can house offices, but they are uncomfortable and alienating as apartments and seldom change over to domestic use. Moreover they vandalize the street and the town in which they stand, casting day-long shadows all around. They change townscape to moonscape, and replace dwelling by moving on. The resulting slap in the face is not merely an aesthetic offence: it is an ecological disaster, driving people to the suburbs and massively contributing to the centrifugal momentum of the townscape.

More recent developments involve an assault not only on the façade, but on the whole idea of public space. Many postmodernist buildings are designed as gadgets – 'so-called objects', as Léon Krier calls them,[18] like the magnified kitchen appliance designed by Morphosis that stands in New York's Cooper Square (Figure 20). The effect of this on the street is catastrophic – compare it with the dignified building to the left of it, but notice too the somewhat similar or at least equally offensive building which stands arbitrarily next to it. To clean the windows of this building you need to block the road with a boom lift. And because it looks like junk it soon will be junk, as the cost of maintenance outstrips the cost of pulling it down and starting again.

This kind of gadget architecture is springing up all over our world: architecture designed at the computer, as a self-contained and context-despising object that has neither scale, materials nor vocabulary in common with its neighbours. Such buildings are without faces, have no privileged orientation, and indeed do not belong where they stand, any more than a space-ship 'belongs' in the precise point of space that it momentarily occupies. Their 'gadget' character is an attempt to borrow the aesthetic of the domestic utensil: they open up the city in the way a tin-opener opens a can. Their effect is to remake the exterior space of the city as a place of discarded interiors – of household junk thrown out in the street. This is the 'me' feeling, without the I that offers an account, or the you that receives it. Such buildings cannot stand happily next to other buildings, for the simple reason that they do not

18. Léon Krier, *Architecture: Choice or Fate*, London, Papadakis, 1998.

Figure 20. Morphosis: Cooper Square, New York.

stand at all. They are designed as waste – throw-away architecture involving vast quantities of energy-intensive materials,
which cannot easily change its function and which will be
demolished within 20 years. Townscapes built from such
architecture resemble land-fill sites – scattered heaps of plastic
junk where no-one settles.

What I am referring to here is the equivalent in architectural
practice of the cancelling of the human face that I commented
on in the last chapter. Gadget architecture neither stands nor
looks: it is dropped in the townscape like litter, and neither
faces the passer-by nor includes him. It may offer shelter, but
it cannot make a home. And by becoming habituated to it
we lose one fundamental component in our respect for the
earth. The gadget building is also a consumer product. It is
to be thrown away once used, and retains its appearance of
stagnant impermanence, like rubbish that no-one has the

responsibility to clear. In this it contributes to the widespread cancellation of the public sphere. Squares and streets are ceasing to be places in which we walk and converse; instead they are places that we hurry through, on our way to a home that we may never find. The gadget requires a clearing around itself; it cannot stand 'next' to anything – the whole idea of 'next' is cancelled by its unmatchable forms. It is an assault on the very principle of neighbourhood – and its facelessness is a denial of neighbour-love.

What all such examples show, however, is that environmental degradation comes in just the same way that moral degradation comes, through de-facing things – representing people and places in impersonal ways, as objects to be used rather than as subjects to be respected. But, the reader may say, the environment *is* only an object or a collection of objects. It is at best a metaphor, at worst a superstition, to think that there is a spirit in the things around us, which we might address and from which we might take consolation, as we address and are consoled by each other. Of course poets and painters have *presented* nature in this way, in the manner of Wordsworth, Hölderlin and Samuel Palmer. But for us this is only a manner of speaking or of seeing – a way of under-lining our emotional dependence on the things around us. Even Rilke's passionate address to the earth, as '*Du liebe*', is no more than an *offer* of subjectivity, a promise to dissolve the earth in the I of the poet.

Or is it so simple? The sense of beauty puts a brake upon destruction, by representing its object as irreplaceable. When the world looks back at me with my eyes, as it does in aesthetic experience, it is also addressing me in another way. Something is being revealed to me, and I am being made to stand still and absorb it. It is of course nonsense to suggest that there are naiads in the trees and dryads in the groves. What is revealed to me in the experience of beauty is a funda-mental truth about being – the truth that being is a gift, and receiving it is a task. This is a truth of theology that demands exposition as such. Hence our exploration of the face of the earth guides us to the real topic of my argument, which is the face of God.

6

The Face of God

Human beings suffer from loneliness in every circumstance of their earthly lives. They can be lonely on their own, or lonely in company; they can enter a crowded room of friendly people only to find their loneliness deepened by it; they can be lonely even in the company of a friend or spouse. There is a human loneliness that stems from some other source than the lack of companionship, and I have no doubt that the mystics who have meditated on this fact are right to see it in metaphysical terms. The separation between the self-conscious being and his world is not to be overcome by any natural process. It is a supernatural defect, which can be remedied only by grace.

That is the conclusion to which I have reluctantly come, and in this chapter I want to complete my argument about the face, by saying something about the presence of God in this world, and why our failure to find him is the cause of such deep disquiet. The position to which I am drawn has been expressed by many thinkers. But every attempt to state it seems to run into logical and metaphysical difficulties. Maybe there is no way to state the position that is not fatally flawed. Writers who see the existential loneliness of man as I see it – as a longing to be dissolved in the subjectivity of God – have written in ways so obscure that I have real doubts whether I can do any better. I am thinking of Kierkegaard, Levinas and Berdyaev, and also of Hegel, in whose shadow they wrote, and whose vision they confirmed by the very vehemence of their attacks on it.

Hegel argued that we self-conscious beings *become what we essentially are*, through a process of conflict and resolution. Self-consciousness is implanted in us as a condition *to be realized*, and we acquire it through *Entäusserung* – through building the public arena in which the dialogue between self and other can occur. The self becomes real through the recognition of the other. Language, institutions, laws are the vehicles through which we achieve *Selbstbestimmung*, the certainty of self, which is also a limiting of self and a recognition of the boundary between self and other.

The process that leads me to see myself as other to others also makes me other to myself, and this is the 'moment', to use Hegel's language, of self-alienation, in which subjects become strangers to themselves, bound by external laws, hampered in their freedom and in rebellion against the constraints that press on them from outside.

It is in this way that the fatal fracture splits our world – the fracture between subject and object that *runs through me*. Healing that fracture means reconciling my own view from somewhere with the competing views by which I am surrounded, so that how I am in the eyes of others matches how I am for myself. For Hegel this is achieved objectively through law and institutions, subjectively through art and religion. These are ways in which we re-connect with the world from which our own struggle for freedom and self-knowledge had separated us. Hölderlin expressed some of this in his great invocations of home and homecoming – the journey outwards, which is also a journey back. And Hölderlin's spiritual journey has been traced in our time, and through a changed emotional geography, by T. S. Eliot in *Four Quartets*.

To the religious person the journey out into alienation (which Jews and Christians capture in the story of original sin and our expulsion from Paradise) demands the journey onwards into redemption. This demand is recorded by St Augustine in his famous words: 'our hearts are restless, until they rest in You' (*Confessions* 1, 1). And it is recorded by the Sufi mystics in their invocation of the final unity with the source of light granted to the *murshid*, or spiritual leader. Indeed many of the great religions seem to have the structure of the Hegelian dialectic: an original innocence, in which the soul is at one with the world and its creator; a 'fall' or rebellion, in which the soul 'realizes' itself as a free individual and is also sundered from its true fulfilment, and a final homecoming through discipline and sacrifice, to be once again in harmony with the cosmos – redeemed by the saviour, released into Nirvana, in the arms of Brahman, or just asleep with the ancestors in the final place of rest.

The metaphysical loneliness of the subject is not a historically transient condition. It is a human universal. As I have argued, the creature with 'I' thoughts is accountable to others, and sees himself from outside, as an other in others' eyes. The endless striving to unite the self who judges with the other who is judged *is* the religious way of life, and all the great religions are formulae for conducting this strife, through which we seek to be 'restored by that refining fire/ Where you must move in measure, like a dancer'. Each religion promises one-ness with the cosmos; each describes the way of piety and obedience; each distinguishes the pure from the impure; and each abounds in sacred times, places and rites, through which the eternal can be encountered in time and through which the individual can be purified and redeemed. Each wraps the individual in the comforts of an enduring community. And all these features of religion are natural consequences of the metaphysical condition that compels us – the condition of creatures who must account for what they are and do, and who look around them for the place where forgiveness and acceptance can be earned and received.

Religion therefore begins in the experience of community, and in the desire to be reconciled with those who judge us and on whose love we depend. I have argued that guilt, shame and remorse are necessary features of the human condition. They are the residue of our mistakes and the sign that we are free to make them. But they direct us towards a higher form of reconciliation – a reconciliation in which our guilt is comprehensively acknowledged and forgiven. For the atheist this aspiration must be either suppressed, or turned in a stoical direction – the direction of the one who wills what is fated, and so achieves another kind of unity between himself and the world. For the religious being, however, redemption is an emancipation from the things of this world, and an identification with a transcendental 'I AM'. For the one who trusts in God this is the consolation for human woes. Our sufferings stem from the burden of responsibility that we assume in our membership of the community of persons. Guilt is the price of our subject-hood, and God's subject-hood is its cure.

As I have argued, this is not just a deluded way of interpreting ordinary fears and desires. It is an attempt to see our relation to the world as we see our relation to each other – as *reaching through* the tissue of objects to the thing that they mean. I have suggested that we extend this way of relating beyond the society of our fellows to the whole of nature, finding subjectivity enfolded, as it were, in the world around us. If there is such a thing as the real presence of God among us, that is how his presence must be understood: not as an abstract system of law, but as a subjective view that takes in the world as a whole. And in this view from nowhere we are judged, as we are judged by every 'I' that turns its face to us. It is through seeing the world and each other in this way that we develop as self-conscious beings, and as we develop ourselves so do we develop around us the external forms of our inner freedom – the social networks, institutions, and laws; the works of art, buildings and landscapes that are the face of our world.

But this means that religions are inseparable from the communities of the faithful. Without the community the real presence of the other is never granted; and without rites of passage and rituals of worship a community cannot become a settlement, attached to the earth and responsible for maintaining it. This leads to a deep problem: how can a religion defend its theological legacy on the grounds of truth, when it must also defend it as a communal possession and a test of membership? Is there not a fundamental conflict here, between the demands of reason and the demands of social cohesion? And if there is not, is it only because we have defined the community so widely that faith is no longer relevant or because we have made faith, as in Islam, the definition of a universal *ummah*, to which we all by nature belong?

As I argued in the first chapter, I regard those questions as serious obstacles to be overcome, by anyone who wishes to reconcile the practice of science with the claims of religion. And they can be answered to the satisfaction of faith, it seems to me, only if we regard the experience of community as a *preparation* for the experience of God, and the experience of God as a *revelation* granted in response to it.

Modern moral philosophy recognizes that personhood is a central category, and also that personhood is a relational idea: you are a person to the extent that you can participate in a network of inter-personal relationships. To be a person, therefore, you must have the capacities that make those relationships possible – some of which I have been discussing in this book. Persons fall under the scope of Kant's moral law: they must respect each other as ends in themselves. In other words, they should grant to each other a sphere of sovereignty. Within your sphere of sovereignty what is done, and what happens to you, in so far as it depends on human choices, depends on choices of yours. This can be guaranteed only if people are shielded from each other by a wall of rights. Without rights individuals are not sovereigns but subjects; and these rights are 'natural' in that they are inherent in the condition of personhood, and not derived from any convention or agreement.

All of that seems, to the modern philosopher, like so much common sense, and a vindication of the life in freedom that is one of the most important legacies of the European Enlightenment. But it leads not only to the privatization of the religious need, but also to a peculiarly bloodless vision of community – one in which 'conceptions of the good', as Rawls describes them, are likewise removed from the public arena and privatized.[1] The abstract liberal concept of the person, as a centre of free choice, whose will is sovereign, and whose rights determine our duties towards him, delivers at best only a part of moral thinking. Persons can be harmed in ways that are not adequately summarized in the idea of a violation of rights. They can be polluted, desecrated, defiled – and in many cases this disaster takes a bodily form. If we don't see this, then not only will sexual morality appear opaque to us and inexplicable; we will lose sight of the ways in which the moral life is lived through the body and displayed in the face.

Many of our moral obligations are chosen, and fall in the public domain of justice and contract. But the obligations on which the enduring community depends are destinies. They are obligations of piety – the ancient *pietas* which, for many Roman thinkers, identified the true core of religious practice and of the religious frame of mind and which, in the easy-going temper of the Augustan age, seemed scarcely to require a belief in the gods or in anything beyond the natural order.

Piety is a posture of submission and obedience towards authorities that you have never chosen. The obligations of

1. See *A Theory of Justice*, Oxford, 1971.

piety, unlike the obligations of contract, do not arise from the consent to be bound by them. They arise from the ontological predicament of the individual. Consider filial obligations. I did not consent to be born from and raised by this woman. I have not bound myself to her by a contract, and there is no knowing in advance what my obligation to her at any point might be or what might fulfil it. The Confucian philosophy places enormous weight on obligations of this kind – obligations of 'Li' – and regards a person's virtue as measured almost entirely on the scale of piety. The ability to recognize and act upon unchosen obligations indicates a character more deeply imbued with trustworthy feeling than the ability to make deals and bide by them – such is the thought. As Cordelia puts it, when unjustly asked to rewrite a bond of piety as a contractual deal: 'According to my bond, no more, no less'.

Piety connects us to the sacred and the sacramental. Pious sentiments gather round moments of sacrifice, in which people devote themselves, undertaking obligations that are too vast or indeterminate to be contained within a contract. These moments are connected with birth, initiation, sexual union and death. They are moments in which the tribe has an interest of its own, as great as the interest of the individual. Marriages belong with Christenings, Bar Mitzvahs and funerals, to the ceremonies that anthropologists, following Van Gennep, have grouped together as 'rites of passage', moments, as Durkheim describes them, of 'social effervescence'.[2] In all societies rites of passage have a religious character. They are episodes in which the dead and the unborn are present, and in which the gods take a consuming interest, sometimes attending in person. In these moments time stands still; or rather they are peculiarly timeless. The passage from one condition to another occurs outside time – as though the participants

2. Arnold Van Gennep, *Les rites de passage*, Paris, Émile Nourry, 1909.

bathe themselves for a moment in eternity and return cleansed to the temporal order.

This way of understanding rites of passage, as sacraments, should not surprise us. For these are moments in which individuals assume the full burden of responsibility, before the eyes of those who will hold them to account for what they are and do. There are plenty of things that an evolutionary psychologist can say, by way of explaining why such moments might have been protected and selected for. But my interest is in the intentionality of the emotions that arise within them. These moments are understood, by the participants, as sacred, and in the concept of the sacred we have a clue not merely to the distinctiveness of the human condition, but also to the religious need that animates it. Evolutionary explanations of our deep desires and deep refusals are indifferent to their intentionality. From the evolutionary point of view it is indeterminate whether incest, for example, should be physically disgusting, like faeces, or a violation of the moral law like theft, or a desecration of the home like gross rudeness. Any of those ways of thinking would ensure that the revulsion against incest is 'selected for'. Evolutionary explanations will therefore tell us nothing about concepts like piety, purity and the sacred, which must be invoked to define the specific intentionality of the incest taboo.

The idea of the sacred influences our response to sexual behaviour, to the rites of passage of the community, and to the moments of consecration in which the deep solemnity of the human condition is rehearsed and condoned. Rather than suggest a biological genealogy of this idea, I would propose instead a metaphysical foundation. The idea of the sacred is attached to times and places in which the real presence of the subject comes vividly into view, so that we sense a bottomless chasm in the scheme of things, a falling away into the transcendental, and ourselves as poised on the edge. This is what happens, it seems to me, in sex and death – at least when they are properly contained and focused by prohibitions, so as to ensure that it is the subject and not the object that is targeted.

In seeing places, buildings and artefacts as sacred we in effect project on to the material world the experience that we receive from each other, when incarnation becomes a 'real presence', and we perceive the other as forbidden to us and untouchable. Hence sexual desire provides us with some of the primary material from which the experience of the sacred is constructed. That was why it appealed to Wagner, as the core subject of his music dramas.

Death too presents us with the mystery of our incarnation, though it does so in another way. In death we confront the body voided of the soul, an object without a subject, limp, ungoverned and inert. The awe that we feel in the face of death is a response to the unfathomable spectacle of human flesh without the self. In fact, the dead body is not so much an object as a void in the world of objects – something that ought not to be there, since it ought not to be there as a thing. The sight is uncanny, *unheimlich*, and demands to be rearranged – though rearranged metaphysically, as it were, so as to heal the void. Hence in all societies the dead are treated with reverence: they become untouchable, precisely in the moment when the self retreats from them. Somehow this body still belongs to the person who has vanished: I imagine him as exerting his claim over it, but from spectral regions where he cannot be touched. In encountering death, therefore, our imagination reaches spontaneously towards the supernatural. The dead body, by becoming sacred, exposes itself also to desecration – a fact upon which the drama of *Antigone* turns. Just as sex and death provide us with two of our primary experiences of the sacred, therefore, they also present us with a primary threat of desecration.

That tentative theory of the sacred is not a piece of empirical anthropology; nor is it an exercise in genealogy, of the kind given by René Girard in his account of ritual sacrifice. According to Girard, all societies are embroiled in conflict, due to the 'mimetic desire' of their members.[3] This rivalry through imitation threatens to blow the community apart, and traps its members into cycles of revenge. In every community, however, there are those who are marked out as Other by some existential fault, such as incest, kingship, *hubris* or some similar sign of ontological 'apartness'. By selecting such a person as victim and putting him to death the community can escape the cycle of revenge. Hence his death, in an act of communal sacrifice, will focus and assuage the existing hostilities, and bring peace and reconciliation to his murderers – who won't be murderers at all, but innocent members of a renewed and purified community. Then, Girard argues, the communal sigh of relief will be projected onto the dead victim, who will be regarded as an offering, a thing of infinite worth, a precious redeemer who must be thanked and revered. This is the primal emotion, according to Girard, from which our sense of the sacred derives. And subsequently this sense spreads to embrace all the rituals and objects that are connected with the act of sacrifice.

That genealogy of the sacred is intriguing, but like so many genealogies it begs the principal question. For it can explain the acquisition of a sense of the sacred only by assuming that people already possess it. The awe that the original community directs towards the sacrificial victim is not any kind of awe. It is the awe owed to sacred things – things held apart and untouchable. What explains *that* emotion? This is surely the question that the genealogy sets out to answer, and which it fails to answer. By contrast the explanation I have given is not a 'myth of origins'. It is a piece of philosophy, an attempt to derive the intentionality of religious awe *a priori*, from the Kantian metaphysic upon which I have been relying

3. *La violence et le sacré*, Paris, Bernard Grasset, 1972.

throughout my argument. It is not, I venture to suggest, the act of *sacrifice* that generates the awe surrounding the scapegoat. It is death, and the moment of death. We look with awe on the human body from which the life has fled. This is no longer a person, but the 'mortal remains' of a person. And this thought fills us with a sense of the uncanny. We may be reluctant to touch the dead body; we see it as in some way not properly a part of our world, as though it has departed from us into another sphere where it cannot be reached.

This experience demands from us a kind of ceremonial recognition. The dead body is the object of rituals and acts of purification, designed not just to send its former occupant happily into the hereafter – for these practices are engaged in even by those who have no belief in the hereafter – but in order to overcome the eeriness, the supernatural quality, of the dead human form. The body is being reclaimed for this world, by the rituals which acknowledge that it stands apart from it. The rituals, to put it in another way, consecrate the body, and purify it of its miasma. Hence they may be the subject matter of a sacred duty, one that eclipses all rival duties, as in the *Antigone* of Sophocles.

In dealing with the dead body, we are in some way standing at the horizon of our world, in direct but ineffable contact with that which does not belong to it. That, I venture to suggest, is the essence of the sacred. And the experience of the sacred needs no theological commentary in order to invade us. It is, in some way, a *primitive* experience, as basic as pain, fear or exultation, awaiting a theological commentary perhaps, but in itself the inevitable precipitation of self-consciousness, which compels us to live forever on the edge of things, present in the world, but also apart from it.

Only that which is sacred can be desecrated. Hence the habitual desecration of death and sexual love are, I venture to suggest, proofs of their sacred nature. And in a culture which is in full flight from the sacred, the practice of desecration becomes a kind of moral necessity – something that must be constantly performed, and performed collectively, in order to destroy the things that stand in judgement over us. All around us, therefore, we find a relentless habit of 'objectification': the display of human beings and their settlements as objects to be consumed and disposed of, the reduction of sex to a relation between body parts, and the display of death in images of crazed destruction, such as those presented in the films of Quentin Tarantino. The rule of the Greek tragic theatre was that death should take place off-stage, to be reported by the chorus or a messenger. It was not squeamishness that dictated this rule (what could be more gruesome than the death of Pentheus as the chorus recounts it in Euripides' *Bacchae*?). The rule was dictated by the deep emotions that death invites, the sacred aura of the victim, and the real meaning of tragedy for us, the survivors. In tragedy death is *faced*; in the violent cinema of today it is defaced. Moreover, we have acquired the habit of defacing not merely the human form but all those aspects of our world in which we recognize that we are called to account. And the explanation is simple: we no longer trust in the intentionality of our sacramental attitudes: they reach out to the sacred, but they do not find it. No God, we believe, reaches down to meet the arms that reach for him, and our arms fall helpless to our sides.

Hence the question that comes immovably into the centre of my discussion is that of the face of God. Granted the intentionality of our 'immortal longings', what can we say about their epistemology? Is there any way of reasoning from our experience in this world to the conclusion that God is immanent within it, or must all this remain an 'as if', whose epistemological failings are supplemented, if at all, only by faith and never by reason?

Certain religious and mystical thinkers have claimed direct experience of God, and their accounts have been gener-alized by Rudolf Otto in his theory of the 'numinous': the '*mysterium tremendum et fascinans*' which evades our ability to describe it, and which is identified by those who experience it as an intrusion into this world from an indescribable reality beyond it.[4] Undoubtedly there are experiences of which we can make sense only by referring them to the transcendental. The experience of being 'in God's hands', of being absolutely safe, which can come as a sudden gift or blessing even in the moment of supreme danger – this is well known in the literature, and no doubt known to many readers of this book. The experience of being guided, impeded, encouraged by an all-observing person: this too is familiar. And even for those who have not encountered God in this way, there is that other and more desolating thing, the sense of guilt and pollution, which can come like a cloud across our lives.

Undoubtedly there are such experiences. But – as Otto's language conveys – they do not contain the proof of their own veracity. Nor can we ascertain, by any empirical enquiry, what these experiences are experiences *of*. Reverting for a moment to the thoughts expounded in the first chapter: no science could ever connect such experiences with a transcendental reality, for the simple reason that science is about causal relations between objects. A causal explanation of the *mysterium tremendum* might connect the experience with disorders of the digestive system or with some neurological disturbance induced by fasting and prayer. But to describe the experience as an encounter with the transcendental is automatically to put it outside the reach of causal reasoning.

Nevertheless, as William James showed in *The Varieties of Religious Experience* – a book derived from one of the earliest series of Gifford lectures – that is how the experience is understood by the subjects themselves. The philosophical question is not whether we can connect the experience of the

4. *Das Heilige*, 1917, trans. as *The Idea of the Holy*, Oxford, Oxford University Press, 1923.

'numinous' case by case with some transcendental origin – for that is impossible – but whether we can present a picture of the world that enables us to *interpret* the religious experience in that way. If we can get this far, then we have made way for the only thing that can sustain the truth of what we feel, which is trust in a personal God who reveals himself.

It is worth dwelling on this point, since it seems to be so completely misunderstood in the current debates between atheists and theists. Explanation by cause and effect involves the discovery of law-like connections between events. The concepts in terms of which those laws are framed are concepts of objects – particles, fields and forces, situated within the space–time continuum. Subjects have no place in those laws, not because they are mysterious or supernatural, but because they exist only *for* each other, through the web of inter-personal accountability. Look for them in the world of objects and you will not find them. This is true of you and me; and it is true too of God. Physics gives a *complete* explanation of the world of objects, for that is what 'physics' means. God is not a 'hypothesis' to be set beside the fundamental constants and the laws of quantum dynamics. Look for him in the world of objects and you will not find him, just as you will not find human freedom with a brain scan, the self with a microscope or a sake in the bath.

That observation takes us back to the topic from which I began: the topic of contingent being. The idea of 'being *qua* being', as Aristotle and Aquinas put it, has received a fairly bad press among more recent philosophers. Kant's attack on the ontological argument, Frege's theory of the existential quantifier, and Quine's account of ontological relativity all feed into the now orthodox view that there is no such topic as being *qua* being. We can describe what it is to be a giraffe or a pop song; but not what it is to *be* simpliciter. Any account of being would presuppose itself, since it would have to assume that we understood what it means to attribute being to the entities referred to in the account. If you don't think that is sufficient proof, then just look at the reams of nonsense poured out by Heidegger, Rahner and others, on the topic. Heidegger has much to say to us, but it is only obscured, in my view, by the invention of Being in its many varieties – in-advance-of-itself-being, being-to-hand, being-towards-death, and so on – as though being were a kind of property, that you might possess at one moment, and lose at the next.

And yet, is there not, after all, a 'question of being'? Or perhaps more than one question? The God of the philosophers entered my argument in response to the question of contingent being. 'Why *is* there anything?' seems like a cogent question. Of course, if we construe the question as asking for a cause, then it may well *not* be cogent. For it would be asking for a cause of the space–time continuum itself, i.e. for a cause of the system of causes, which is not an item within that system and therefore not a cause. In other words it would be a question that can be answered only by a self-contradiction. But this is not how the question is understood by those who have traditionally asked it. Theologians have been seeking for a 'ground of Being', in other words, for an entity that provides a *reason* for the whole of things, rather than a cause. It is not causation but revelation that leads us to such an entity – the kind of revelation that I have been describing in this book.

Being is bound to be a puzzle for us. To explain the being of one thing is always to assume the being of another: and either the regress is infinite or being presents us, somewhere, somehow, with its own rationale. Such a rationale would take us out of the empirical world – the world of scientific investigation – so as to obtain what Kant says to be impossible, the transcendental perspective, the view from nowhere, which embraces the world as a whole. We have the idea of this perspective, however, and often we feel that we can understand the being of things – of individual things and of the totality of things – because we have been able to understand being as something *granted*. Through meditating on being in that way, we glimpse a path out of the system of causes to a relational picture of the world – a picture of the world as standing in relation to something revealed within it.

Aquinas argued that being is characterized by three features: truth, unity and goodness. These three features, because they belong to everything real, he called 'transcendentals'.[5] That is to say, their presence cannot be explained by some specific or local condition of things, but only by reference to the world as a whole. Maybe there is a fourth transcendental – beauty. But at any rate, there are these three. And we understand being as that which is coextensive with truth, unity and goodness. Everything that is – every being – is also true, one and good. (Aquinas adopted the standard medieval view that evil is not being but privation.) God wills the being of things – that is what his love consists in. Hence he wills truth, unity and goodness in all their varied realizations.

To a modern reader it often seems as if all this is going round in circles, using one abstraction to replace another until we come back to where we started. But a sympathetic reading of Aquinas would suggest, rather, that he is showing the deep connection between the world of contingencies, and the world of values. Being presents us with unified individuals, and therefore with plenitude; it presents us with truth, and therefore with knowledge; and it presents us with goodness, and therefore with the end or purpose of the world. These are *a priori* features of being, and ways in which being *makes itself known to us*.

It is not only Christian thinkers who have sought for a key to the mystery of being. The Hindus believe that, case by case, we can find our way to the subjectivity of objects, so as to understand each being from within, as a manifestation of the *atman*, the 'self of the world'. That which had appeared

5. *Disputed Questions on Truth*, q1 a1.

arbitrary is referred, instead, to the being upon which all depends. Being then makes sense to us, not as mere being, nor as 'being there', but as 'being given'. We receive the world as a gift, by relating it to the transcendental subjectivity, the primordial 'I', in which each thing occurs as a free thought. It seems to me that this is the message of religion in all its forms: and we come to understand it by encountering the spirit of gift within ourselves.

In the religions that are familiar to us, the idea of grace is of fundamental importance. The term (Latin *gratia*) translates a variety of words in Hebrew, Greek, Arabic and Sanskrit, but all our sacred texts seem to point in the same direction, affirming that God's relation to the world as a whole, and to each of us in particular, is one of *giving*. The beseeching of God's grace is the central feature of the Anglican liturgy. The great prayer of the Catholic Church, based on a poem in the New Testament, greets the Virgin Mary with the words 'Hail Mary, full of Grace, blessed art thou among women, and blessed is the fruit of thy womb, Jesus'. The Koran opens with the verse that forms a refrain in the life of all Muslims: *bism illah il-raHmân il-raHîm*, in the name of God, full of grace, full of graciousness, as Mohamed Asad translates it, and the root *rHm* is shared with Hebrew, used often in the Old Testament to denote God's concern for us, his recognition of our weakness, and his abundance of gifts. The idea that the world is sustained by gift is second nature to religious people, who believe that they should be givers in their turn, if they are to receive the gift on which they depend for their salvation.

As I argued in Chapter Four, *agape* does not raise us *to* God, but comes down to us *from* God. It is received as a gift, and then distributed by each of us to our neighbours, as another gift. Hence C. S. Lewis, in *The Four Loves*, called it 'gift-love'. It fills the world with the spirit of gift – but not a personal, exclusive or jealous gift, like erotic love. It is a gift that makes no demands; *agape* pursues the interest of the other and not that of the self. Mephistopheles describes himself to Faust as *der Geist der stets verneint*, the spirit that always negates. Just so is *agape* the opposite – the spirit that always affirms, by following the path of gift and sacrifice. Through *agape* we overcome the guilt of our own existence; we recognize that contingency brings suffering, and that suffering is a call to sacrifice. This spiritual transformation, whereby we come to accept both suffering and sacrifice, and find in them the moral order that makes sense of our lives, is rightly described as a 'redemption'.

There is surely a great difference, which we all understand, between seeing something as just *there* (there for the taking) and seeing it as a gift. Only what is owned can be given, and gifts therefore come wrapped in the perspective of the giver, who has claimed them as 'mine', and also relinquished that claim for another's sake. And the one who receives something as a gift receives it as a mark of the other's concern for him; gratitude is not just normal – it is the recognition that the thing has really been given, and is not the first step in a bargain. Gifts involve conscious reflection on self and other, on rights and duties, on ownership and its transcendence. Hence they can only be offered I to I, and gifts are acts of acknowledgement between persons, in which each recognizes the freedom of the other. What looks like gift in other species is something else: for example, an instinctive withdrawal in favour of a kin-related member of the herd. And as I argued earlier, those evolutionary psychologists who describe the genetically motivated 'altruism' of animals in the language of human self-sacrifice overlook what is most distinctive of the human case, which is the decision to sacrifice oneself for the sake of another. I earlier remarked that it is as nonsensical to speak of the self as an object as it is to speak in the same way of a sake. Perhaps it is worth adding that only a self can understand a sake, and that to make sacrifices for others' sake is to walk with God.

The religious frame of mind involves two 'moments' – as Hegel might put it. There is the moment of communion, and the moment of gift. The religious person is the one who experiences the deep need to give thanks; and he experiences this need as a communal impulse, something that he shares and which brings him together with a community, even if only a would-be community, a 'communion of saints' whose 'Holy City' has yet to be realized on earth. His need to give thanks is not circumstantial but metaphysical. It is rooted in the experience of being itself, in his way of understanding what it is to be. Being, for the religious person, is a gift, not a fact. It is through understanding this that we overcome our metaphysical loneliness, and understanding may require privation and suffering, through which we discard the dross of our own distractions. Hence the world, and the objects contained in it, come before the religious consciousness as the signs of another perspective – the perspective that has 'given these things to me'. That perspective, which the Hindus call Brahman, is hidden from us in the way every other 'I' is hidden. But like those other 'I's it can appear in our world as a *real presence*. The gathering together of the community in the moment of thanks prepares the way for this.

The most important occasions for communal thanks are the ceremonies in which social membership is renewed. For the participants the rite of passage is an enhanced experience of being, in which the aspect of gift is emphasized and solemnized. Birth is a gift of new life; the rite of initiation is a gift of the world and its knowledge to the youth and of the youth to the tribe; marriage is a gift of two people to each other, in which others participate with gifts; the funeral is a service of thanks for a life, and a ritual mourning for someone whose life is thereby replayed in retrospect as a giving, its previous character as a 'taking' entirely expunged.

Gift lies at the heart of sacrificial religion too. The offering at the altar is a gift to the god, who himself returns it as a gift to his worshippers. There is a mysterious feeling of unity that is experienced by the worshippers at this moment – the moment of the sacrament, when what is given is also received, but received in another form. All sacred moments are moments of gift – of gift revealed as *the way things are*. The distinctiveness of the Christian Eucharist is that it makes this wholly specific. The Eucharist commemorates God's supreme gift, which is the gift of himself – his own descent into the world of suffering and guilt, in order to show through his example that there is a way out of conflict and resentment – a way to restore through grace the givenness of the world.

For me the Christian view of the matter is the one that gives the greatest insight into our situation. The Christian God is *agape*, and even in a world that has launched itself on the path of desecration, he can show himself in the sacrificial acts of individual people, when they set aside the call of self-interest and act for others' sake. Acts of self-sacrifice appear in the world of objects and causes as revelations: the I that gives itself opens a window in the scheme of things through which we glimpse the light beyond – the I AM that spoke to Moses.

God revealed himself on that occasion as we do – by coming to the threshold of himself. He came before Moses as a point of view, a first person perspective, the transcendental 'I am' that cannot be known as an object but only as a subject. This perspective can become a real presence among us only if it can be revealed in the world of objects, as the human subject is revealed in the human face. But how can this be?

Christianity has an answer to that question and that answer is the incarnation. God, in the person of Christ, is present among us. It is from the life of Christ that we can understand the true nature of God's goodness. Christians believe that, in undergoing crucifixion, Christ took the sufferings of the world on himself – in other words, he lifted suffering out of the negativity in which we tend to view it, and showed it as an attribute of God, something which is not, therefore, alien to the world of creation but an integral part of it. Through suffering Christ showed us that our own suffering is worthwhile, and the occasion through which to grow morally by imitating him. By making himself available for suffering, so to speak, God could make a gift of himself in Christ, a sacrifice which points us towards salvation, by showing that sacrifice is what life on earth is all about.[6]

The power of this idea is evident. It makes the real presence of God easy to understand, because it becomes merely a special case of the real presence of the human subject (an experience that independently dominates the lives of human beings). But it leaves us with a residual concept – that of the Incarnation – every bit as puzzling and mysterious as the one that it set out to explain: a concept that once again lies inexplicably suspended between causation and revelation. So is this as far as we can get? Perhaps it is, from the metaphysical point of view. But from the moral point of view there are a few thoughts to be added, which are thoughts that are as relevant for an atheist as they are for a believer. Indeed it was a non-believer who gave them their deepest expression.

When Wagner set out to write *The Ring of the Nibelung* he was not a Christian, but an agnostic, heavily influenced by Feuerbach's projectionist account of religion in general and Christianity in particular.[7] But he asked himself an interesting question that Feuerbach had ignored, which is this. Suppose the gods are our invention, made in our own image, infused

---

6. See the illuminating account by Max Scheler, 'The Meaning of Suffering', in Max Scheler, *On Feeling, Knowing and Valuing*, trans. Harold J. Bershady, Chicago, University of Chicago Press, 1992.

7. The Feuerbachian allegory that inspired Wagner's original poem and which provides one layer of meaning in a many-layered palimpsest has been authoritatively set out by Paul Heise. See his magisterial analysis of *The Ring* at Wagnerheim.com.

with our own passions like the gods in Homer, but with the additional attribute of ensuring the maintenance of law and order here below. What would those gods need in order to be truly objects of love? Wagner depicts the attempt of Wotan, king of the gods and lord of the world, to achieve the kind of serenity that comes from absolute control of the universe – a universe that preceded his own rise to power, and which obeys its own inscrutable and primeval laws. He shows that Wotan cannot do this without defying the moral law, and that his status as guardian of law and order is a sham. He is not evil, but he lacks something that is necessary to achieve true virtue. Meanwhile, in his attempt to retain the power that he has unjustly acquired, he creates a race of earthly beings who will have the freedom that he himself no longer possesses and who, guided but not compelled by him, will undo the mischief that he had set in motion by wanting to be the supreme ruler of the world.

The human world that he has created is portrayed in *Die Walküre*, as a world of struggle and resentment. But it contains two precious attributes that Wotan himself does not possess, though he has a kind of polished veneer that substitutes for them – the attributes of freedom and love. The freedom of the human being, as Siegmund and Sieglinde exemplify it, is the freedom to defy laws, fate, death itself, for the sake of another – the freedom to make a gift of *oneself*. And this freedom is possible only where there is also suffering, otherwise the gift is costless, and not a genuine sacrifice. Self and sake become one in the moment of sacrifice.

In the second act of *Walküre* we encounter this process of sacrificial gift played out in the character of Siegmund, and in the great stichomythic dialogue between Siegmund and Brünnhilde we see a free mortal, accepting death and suffering out of love for another, confronting a cold-hearted immortal, and awakening in her the sense of what she lacks. Siegmund's questions are framed thus (Example 1):

Example 1

The melody ascends through an octave, as the bass descends by the same measure, carrying with it suspended harmonies that move to a dominant seventh – left unresolved, expectant and petitioning. This epitome of our mortal prayers receives only stony, implacable re-statements of the divine decree. When an answer comes it is Siegmund who provides it:

So jung und schön erschimmerst du mir,
Doch wie kalt und hart erkennt dich mein Herz!

Example 2

And the melody finds its completion in a gesture of defiance (the four-note motive on E, F sharp and G, Example 2) which henceforth dominates the musical line. Siegmund's need enters the soul of Brünnhilde and her façade of divine implacability cracks. He forces her to account for herself and in doing so she confronts him I to I, and so falls into the human world of love and suffering. As her divine façade crumbles, a face appears, and it is a face ready for love and destined for sacrifice. In the third act Brünnhilde prepares herself for the trials of mortality. She throws in her lot with the world of human love. But she will suffer as humans suffer, being used and discarded by the person to whom she has made a gift of her entire self.

The third act of *Walküre* is a profound philosophical reflection on the idea of incarnation, suggesting that the things that we truly value, and which are for us the avenue to meaning, are intimately connected with suffering, and the ability – definitive of our humanity – to accept suffering for the sake of love. Wagner's later works – notably *Tristan* and *Parsifal* – take this theme further. But the dénouement of the *Ring* already depends on the idea that the gods achieve redemption only through accepting the condition of mortality, since only this renders them capable of sacrifice and the love of which sacrifice is the proof. In accepting this they too learn suffering. And through this suffering a god acquires the ability to make a gift of himself, by renouncing life (and therefore immortality).

The Ring can be understood as an attempt to show, through artistic rather than intellectual means, the deep connection between freedom and suffering. It is in terms of this connection that we understand the highest form of love – the love in which giving is total. If God is to enjoy that love, and the redemption that is innate within it, the implication is, then he too must be incarnate in mortal form. Love belongs to the human condition, and God becomes a complete object of love by accepting that condition as his own.

Although, as I remarked, Wagner's plot was conceived against the background of Feuerbach's projectionist account of religious belief, it contains an important moral for believers too. It attempts to show at the deepest emotional level, that all that we truly esteem, love included, depends in the end on suffering, and on our freedom to accept suffering for another's sake. This idea is contained in the motive (Example 3) that occurs twice, once in Sieglinde's thanks for Brünnhilde's barely guessed-at sacrifice, and once at the end of the whole cycle, as the waters of the Rhine settle over the wreckage and nature is restored. Suffering is made available to God himself by the act of incarnation, and it is the way – perhaps the sole way – in which he can show that he loves us with a humanly intelligible love, by suffering for our sakes. How to incorporate that thought into a cogent theology of creation is of course a difficult matter – but in itself it is a perfectly cogent thought, and fundamental to the Christian understanding of our relation to God.

Example 3

So what and where is the face of God for the one who believes in his real presence among us? The answer is that we encounter this presence everywhere, in all that suffers and renounces for another's sake. Things with a face are illuminated by the subjectivity that shines in them, and which spreads around them a halo of prohibitions. When someone enters the moment of sacrifice, throwing away what is most precious, even life itself, for the sake of another, then we encounter the supreme moment of gift. This is an act in which the I appears completely. It is also a revelation. In sacrifice and renunciation the I makes of its own being a gift, and thereby shows us that being *is* a gift. In the moment of sacrifice people come face to face with God, who is present too in those places where sorrow has left its mark or 'prayer has been valid'.

We should not be surprised, therefore, if God is so rarely encountered now. The consumer culture is one without sacrifices; easy entertainment distracts us from our metaphysical loneliness. The rearranging of the world as an object of appetite obscures its meaning as a gift. The defacing of *eros* and the loss of rites of passage eliminate the old conception of human life as an adventure within the community and an offering to others. It is inevitable, therefore, that moments of sacred awe should be rare among us. And it is surely this, rather than the arguments of the atheists, that has led to the decline of religion. Our world contained many openings onto the transcendental; but they have been blocked by waste. You may think that this does not matter – that mankind has had enough of sacred mysteries and their well-known dangers. But I think we are none of us at ease with the result. Our disenchanted life is, to use the Socratic idiom, 'not a life for a human being'. By remaking human beings and their habitat as objects to consume rather than subjects to revere we invite the degradation of both. Postmodern people will deny that their disquiet at these things has a religious meaning. But I hope that my argument has gone some way to showing that they are wrong.

Picture credits

Figure 1.   *The Expression of the Emotions in Man and Animals* three illustrations of aggression by Charles Darwin 1872 (Reproduced with permission from John van Wyhe ed. 2002–. The Complete Work of Charles Darwin Online. (http://darwin-online.org.uk/)

Figure 2.   *Self Portrait* by Rembrandt van Rijn (© akg-images / Eric Lessing)

Figure 3.   *The Artist's Mother* by Rembrandt van Rijn (1606–69), Private Collection (© The Bridgeman Art Library)

Figure 4.   *Eros and Psyche* by Antonio Canova (© Peter Barritt / Alamy)

Figure 5.   *Woman with a Mask* by Lorenzo Lippi. (© The Art Gallery Collection / Alamy)

Figure 6.   *Susanna and the Elders* by Rembrandt van Rijn, The Hague, Mauritshuis (© 2011. Photo Scala, Florence)

Figure 7.   *Brigand Stripping Woman* by Francisco Goya (© akg-images / Album / Oronoz)

Figure 8.   *Expulsion from Paradise* by Masaccio, Florence, Santa Maria del Carmine. (© 2011. Photo Scala, Florence/ Fondo Edifici di Culto – min. dell'Interno)

Figure 9.   Detail of *Smiling Angel*, Reims Cathedral (© JTB Photo Communications, Inc. / Alamy)

Figure 10. Detail of *Ecstasy of Saint Teresa* by Gian Lorenzo Bernini (© Bettmann/CORBIS)

Figure 11. Detail of *Birth of Venus* by Sandro Botticelli (© Classic Image / Alamy)

Figure 12. Detail of *Birth of Venus* by William Bouguereau (1825–1905) Paris, Musee d'Orsay. Oil on canvas (© 2011. Photo Scala, Florence)

Figure 13. Fluted columns (© Craig Lovell / Eagle Visions Photography / Alamy)

Figure 14. Whitby (© Geoff Holdsworth / Alamy)

Figure 15. Los Angeles (© Nik Wheeler / Alamy)

Figure 16. Venice Canal (© Freefoto.com)

Figure 17. Detail of *Wanderer Above a Sea of Fog* by, Caspar David (1774–1840): c. 1817. Hamburg, Hamburger Kunsthalle. Oil on canvas, 94, 8 × 74.8 cm. Inv.: 5161. On Permanent loan from the Foundation for the Promotion of the Hamburg Art Collections. Photo: Elke Walford. © 2011. Photo Scala, Florence/BPK, Bildagentur fuer Kunst, Kultur und Geschichte, Berlin

Figure 18. Bucharest (© Gianni Muratore / Alamy)

Figure 19. *The Adoration of the Golden Calf* by Nicolas Poussin 1633–4. London, National Gallery. Oil on canvas, 153.4 × 211.8 cm. Bought with a contribution from The Art Fund, 1945. Acc.n.: 3559 (© 2011. Copyright The National Gallery, London/Scala, Florence)

Figure 20. Cooper Square, New York

Index of Names

Index of Subjects

184